UNIT 4

MUSICAL INSTRUMENTS AND THE VOICE

50 Ready-to-Use Activities for Grades 3–9

MUSICAL INSTRUMENTS AND THE VOICE

50 Ready-to-Use Activities for Grades 3–9

Audrey J. Adair

Illustrated by Leah Solsrud

MUSIC CURRICULUM ACTIVITIES LIBRARY

Parker Publishing Company, Inc.
West Nyack, N.Y.

© 1987 *by*

PARKER PUBLISHING COMPANY, INC.

West Nyack, N.Y.

Library of Congress Cataloging-in-Publication Data

Adair, Audrey J.
  Musical instruments and the voice.

  (Music curriculum activities library ; unit 4)
  1. School music—Instruction and study. 2. Musical
instruments. 3. Voice. I. Title. II. Series: Adair,
Audrey J.,   Music curriculum activities
library ; unit 4.
MT10.A14 1987 unit 4 373.8'7 s [372.8'73] 87-8834

ISBN 0-13-606963-0

Printed in the United States of America

About the Author

Audrey J. Adair has taught music at all levels in the Houston, Texas, and Dade County, Florida, public schools. She has served as a music consultant, music specialist, general music instructor, choir director, and classroom teacher. In addition, she has written a series of musical programs for assemblies and holiday events, conducted music workshops, organized music programs for the community, established glee club organizations, and done specialization work with gifted and special needs students. Currently, she directs and coordinates children's choirs, performs as soloist with flute as well as voice, and composes sacred music.

Mrs. Adair received her B.A. in Music Education from St. Olaf College in Northfield, Minnesota, and has done graduate work at the University of Houston and Florida Atlantic University in Fort Lauderdale. She is also the author of *Ready-to-Use Music Activities Kit* (Parker Publishing Company), a resource containing over 200 reproducible worksheets to teach basic music skills and concepts.

About the *Library*

The *Music Curriculum Activities Library* was developed for you, the busy classroom teacher and music specialist, to provide a variety of interesting, well-rounded, step-by-step activities ready for use in your music classroom. The *Library*'s seven carefully planned Units combine imagination, motivation, and student involvement to make learning as exciting as going on a field trip and as easy as listening to music.

The units of the *Music Curriculum Activities Library* are designed to be used separately or in conjunction with each other. Each Unit contains 50 *all new* ready-to-use music activity sheets that can be reproduced as many times as needed for use by individual students. These 350 illustrated, easy-to-read activities will turn even your most reluctant students into eager learners. Each Unit offers a wealth of information on the following topics:

Unit 1: *Basic Music Theory* develops an understanding of the basic elements of melody, rhythm, harmony, and dynamics.

Unit 2: *Reading and Writing Music* provides a source of reinforcement and instills confidence in the beginner performer through a wide range of note-reading and writing activities in the treble clef, bass clef, and in the clef of one's own instrument.

Unit 3: *Types of Musical Form and Composition* gives the student the foundation needed to enjoy worthwhile music by becoming acquainted with a wide variety of styles and representative works.

Unit 4: *Musical Instruments and the Voice* provides knowledge of and insight into the characteristic sounds of band, orchestra, folk instruments, and the voice.

Unit 5: *Great Composers and Their Music* familiarizes the student with some of the foremost composers of the past and present and their music; and cultivates an early taste for good music.

Unit 6: *Special Days Throughout the Year* offers the student well-illustrated, music-related activities that stimulate interest and discussion about music through holidays and special occasions for the entire school year.

Unit 7: *Musicians in Action* helps the student examine music as a pastime or for a career by exploring daily encounters with music and the skills, duties, environment, and requirements of a variety of careers in music.

vi

How to Use the *Library*

The activities in each Unit of the *Library* may be sequenced and developed in different ways. The general teacher may want to use one activity after the other, while the music specialist may prefer to use the activities in conjunction with the sequencing of the music curriculum. Teachers with special or individualized needs may select activities from various Units and use them over and over before actually introducing new material.

Let's take a closer look at how you can use the *Music Curriculum Activities Library* in your particular classroom situation:

... For THE MUSIC TEACHER who is accountable for teaching classes at many grade levels, there is a wide range of activities with varying degrees of difficulty. The activity sheets are ideal to strengthen and review skills and concepts suitable for the general music class.

... For THE NEW TEACHER STARTING A GENERAL MUSIC CLASS, these fun-filled activities will provide a well-balanced, concrete core program.

... For THE SPECIALIZED TEACHER who needs to set definite teaching goals, these activities offer a wealth of information about certain areas of music, such as career awareness, composers, and musical forms.

... For THE BAND AND CHOIR DIRECTOR, these activity sheets are a valuable resource to explore band, orchestra, and folk instruments, along with the singing voice.

... For THE PRIVATE MUSIC TEACHER who wants to sharpen and improve students' note reading skills, the *Library* offers ample homework assignments to give students the additional practice they need. There are many activity sheets using the clef of one's instrument and theory pages with illustrations of the keyboard.

... For THE MUSIC CONSULTANT using any one of the units, there are plenty of activities specifically correlated to the various areas of music providing reinforcement of learning. The activity sheets are suitable for class adoption in correlation with any music book series.

... For THE THEORY TEACHER, there are activities to show the students that music analysis is fun and easy.

... For THE TEACHER WHO NEEDS AN ADEQUATE MEANS OF EVALUATING STUDENT PROGRESS, there are fact-filled activities ideal for diagnostic purposes. A space is provided on each sheet for a score to be given.

. . . For THE CLASSROOM TEACHER with little or no musical background, the *Library* offers effective teaching with the flexibility of the seven units. All that has to be done is to decide on the music skill or concept to be taught and then duplicate the necessary number of copies. Even the answers can be duplicated for self-checking.

. . . For THE SUBSTITUTE TEACHER, these sheets are ideal for seatwork assignments because the directions are generally self-explanatory with minimal supervision required.

. . . For THE INSTRUCTOR OF GIFTED STUDENTS, the activities may be used for any type of independent, individualized instruction and learning centers. When used in an individualized fashion, the gifted student has an opportunity to pursue music learning at his or her own pace.

. . . For THE TEACHER OF SPECIAL EDUCATION, even the disadvantaged and remedial student can get in on the fun. Each concept or skill will be mastered as any lesson may be repeated or reinforced with another activity. Some of these activity sheets are designed to provide success for students who have difficulty in other subject areas.

. . . For the INDIVIDUAL who desires to broaden and expand his or her own knowledge and interest in music, each Unit provides 50 activities to help enjoy music.

The *Music Curriculum Activities Library* is ideally a teacher's program because a minimum of planning is required. A quick glance at the Contents in each Unit reveals the titles of all the activity sheets, the ability level necessary to use them, and the skills involved for each student. Little knowledge of music is generally needed to introduce the lessons, and extensive preparation is seldom necessary. You will, of course, want to read through the activity before presenting it to the class. In cases where you need to give information about the activity, two different approaches might be considered. (1) Use the activity as a basis for a guided discussion before completing the activity to achieve the desired results, or (2) Use the activity as a foundation for a lesson plan and then follow up by completing the activity. Either one of these approaches will enhance your own and your students' confidence and, by incorporating a listening or performing experience with this directed study, the students will have a well-rounded daily lesson.

All activity sheets throughout the *Library* have the same format. They are presented in an uncluttered, easy-to-read fashion, with self-explanatory directions. You need no extra materials or equipment, except for an occasional pair of scissors. The classroom or resource area should, however, contain a few reference books, such as song books or music series' books, encyclopedias, reference books about composers, a dictionary, music dictionary or glossary, and so on, so that while working on certain activities the student has easy access to resource books. Then, you simply need to duplicate the activity sheet as many times as needed and give a copy to each student. Even paper grading can be kept to a minimum by reproducing the answer key for self-checking.

The collection of activities includes practice in classifying, matching, listing, researching, naming, drawing, decoding, identifying, doing picture or crossword puzzles, anagrams, word searches, musical word squares, and much much more.

These materials may be used successfully with students in grades 3 and up. The activities and artwork are intentionally structured to appeal to a wide range of ages. For this reason, no grade-level references appear on the activity sheets so that you can use them in a variety of classroom settings, although suggested ability levels (beginner, intermediate, advanced) appear in the Contents.

The potential uses for the *Library* for any musical purpose (or even inter-disciplinary study) are countless. Why? Because these activities allow you to instruct an entire class, a smaller group within the classroom, or individual students. While you are actively engaged in teaching one group of students, the activity sheets may be completed by another group. In any kind of classroom setting, even with the gifted music student or the remedial child, no student needs to sit idle. Now you will have more time for individual instruction.

The Units may be used in a comprehensive music skills program, in an enrichment program, or even in a remedial program. The *Library* is perfect for building a comprehensive musicianship program, improving basic music skills, teaching career awareness, building music vocabulary, exploring instruments, developing good taste in listening to music, appreciating different types of music, creating a positive learning environment, and providing growing confidence in the performer.

What Each Unit Offers You

A quick examination of the **Contents** will reveal a well balanced curriculum. Included are the titles of all activities, the level of difficulty, and the skill involved. The exception to this is Unit 6, where the date and special day, rather than the skill, are listed with the title of each activity.

Each of the **50 reproducible activity sheets** generally presents a single idea, with a consistent format and easy-to-follow directions on how to do the activity, along with a sufficient amount of material to enable the student to become proficient through independent and self-directed work. Because each activity has but one single behavioral objective, mastery of each skill builds confidence that allows the learner to continue progressively toward a more complete understanding of the structure of music, appreciation of music, and its uses. The activity sheets are just the right length, too, designed to be completed within a class period.

The **Progress Chart** provides a uniform, objective method of determining what skills have been mastered. With the aid of this chart, you will be able to keep track of goals, set priorities, organize daily and weekly lesson plans, and track assignments. The Progress Chart lists each activity and skill involved, and has a space for individual names or classes to be recorded and checked when each activity and skill is complete. The Progress Chart is ideal for accurate record keeping. It provides a quick, sure method for you to determine each individual student's achievements or weaknesses.

Use the **Teacher's Guide** for practical guidance on how the particular Unit will work for you. An easy effective learning system, this guide provides background information and reveals new techniques for teaching the Unit.

Throughout the *Library*, each **Answer Key** is designed with a well-thought-out system for checking students' answers. While some activities are self-checking without the use of the Answer Key, other activities can easily be student corrected, too, by simply duplicating the answer page and cutting apart the answers by activity number.

The Self-Improvement Chart provides the student with a self-assessment system that links curriculum goals with individual goals. By means of an appraisal checklist, the chart gives the student and teacher alike the key to finding individual talent. It also measures accountability. Included in the chart are (1) a method for recording goals and acquired music skills; (2) a log for attendance at special music events; (3) a music and instrument check-out record; (4) a log for extra credit activities and music projects; (5) a record of special music recognition awards, incentive badges, Music Share-a-Grams, Return-a-Grams; and (6) a record of music progress.

These specific features of the chart will help you:

- Provide a uniform, objective method of determining rewards for students.
- Assess future curriculum needs by organizing long-term information on student performance.
- Foster understanding of why students did or did not qualify for additional merit.
- Motivate students by giving them feedback on ways for self-improvement.
- Assist students in making statements of their own desires and intentions for learning, and in checking progress toward their goals.

The **Music Share-a-Gram** is a personalized progress report addressed to the parent and created to show the unique qualities of the individual child. It allows you to pinpoint areas of success and tell parents what they need to know about their child. The Music Share-a-Gram evaluates twelve important abilities and personal traits with ratings from exceptional to unsatisfactory, which you might want to discuss with students to solicit their reaction. For example, you might use these ratings as a basis for selecting a student to attend the gifted program in music. This form is designed to be sent with or without the Return-a-Gram, and may be hand-delivered by the student or sent through the mail. For easy record keeping, make a copy of the Gram and attach it to the back of the Student Record Profile Chart.

The **Return-a-Gram** is designed to accompany the Music Share-a-Gram and is sent to the parent on special occasions. When a reply is not expected or necessary, simply detach the Return-a-Gram before sending the Share-a-Gram. This form encourages feedback from the parent and even allows the parent to arrange for a parent-teacher conference. Both Grams are printed on the same page and are self-explanatory—complete with a dotted line for the parent to detach, fill in, and return.

The **Student Record Profile Chart** is a guide for understanding and helping students, and offers a means of periodic evaluation. The chart is easy to use and provides all you need for accurate record keeping and measuring accountability for individual student progress throughout all seven units. It provides an accumulative skills profile for the student and represents an actual score of his or her written performance for each activity. Here is a workable form that you can immediately tailor to your own requirements for interpretation and use of scores. Included are clear instructions, with an example, to help you record your students' assessment on a day-to-day basis, to keep track of pupil progress, and to check learning patterns over a period of time. This chart allows you to spot the potential superior achiever along with the remedial individual. The chart coordinates all aspects of data ranging from the students' name, class, school, classroom teacher's name, semester, date, page number, actual grade, and attendance.

The **Word List** is presented as a reinforcement for building a music vocabulary. It emphasizes the use of dictionary skills; the students make a glossary of important words related to the particular unit. Its purpose is to encourage the use of vocabulary skills by helping develop an understanding of the music terms, concepts, and names found on the activity sheets. This vocabulary reference page is meant to be reproduced and used by the individual student throughout the units as a guide for spelling, word recognition, pronunciation, recording definitions, plus any other valuable information. Throughout six units of the *Library*, a cumulation of the words are presented on the Word List pages. (A Word List is not included in Unit 4.) With the help of this extensive vocabulary, when the student uses the words on both the activity page and the Word List, they will become embedded as part of his or her language.

Each Unit contains a wide-ranging collection of **Incentive Badges**. Use them to reward excellence, commend effort, for bonuses, prizes, behavior modification, or as reminders. These badges are designed to capture the interest and attention of the entire school. Several badges are designed with an open-ended format to provide maximum flexibility in meeting any special music teaching requirement.

Included in each Unit is a simple **Craft Project** that may be created by the entire class or by individual students. Each craft project is an integral part of the subject matter of that particular unit and will add a rich dimension to the activities. The materials necessary for the construction of the craft projects have been limited to those readily available in most classrooms and call for no special technical or artistic skills.

PLUS each Unit contains:

- Worked-out sample problems for students to use as a standard and model for their own work.

- Additional teaching suggestions in the Answer Key for getting the most out of certain activities.

- Extra staff paper for unlimited use, such as composing, ear training, improvising, or writing chords.

- Activities arranged in a sequential pattern.

Resources for Teaching Music More Effectively

- Have a classroom dictionary available for reference.

- Have a glossary or music dictionary available for reference.

- Use only one activity sheet per class session.

- Distribute the Word List prior to the first activity sheet of the particular unit. Encourage students to underline familiar words on the list and write definitions or identifications on the back before instruction on the unit begins. Later, the students can compare their answers with those studied.

- Provide short-term goals for each class session and inform students in advance that awards will be given for the day. You'll see how their conduct improves, too.

- Encourage students to make or buy an inexpensive folder to store music activity sheets, craft projects, word lists, self-evaluation charts, and so on. Folders might be kept in the classroom when not in use and distributed at the beginning of each class period.

- Many of the activities are ideal for bulletin board display. If space is not available to display all students' work, rotate the exhibits.

- Encourage students to re-read creative writing pages for clarity and accuracy before copying the final form on the activity sheet. Proofreading for grammatical and spelling errors should be encouraged.

- For creative drawing activities, encourage students to sketch their initial ideas on another sheet of paper first, then draw the finished product on the activity sheet. It is not necessary to have any technical ability in drawing to experience the pleasure of these creative activities.

- Although you will probably want to work through parts of some activities with your students, and choose some activities for group projects, you will find that most lessons are designed to lead students to the correct answers with little or no teacher direction. Students can be directed occasionally to work through an activity with a partner to search out and correct specific errors.

- Self-corrections and self-checking make a much better impression on young learners than do red-penciled corrections by the classroom music teacher.

- On activities where answers will vary, encourage students to rate their own work on correctness, originality, completeness, carefulness, realism, and organization.

• Most activity pages will serve as a "teacher assistant" in developing specific skills or subject areas to study. The activities throughout the series are complete with learning objectives and are generally factual enough for the teacher to use as a basis for a daily lesson plan.

• The library research activities promote creativity instead of copying while students search out relevant data from a variety of sources, such as encyclopedias, dictionaries, reference books, autobiographies, and others. These activities are ideal for the individual student or groups of students working beyond the classroom environment.

• The following are practical guidelines in planning, organizing, and constructing the Craft Projects:

> . . . Acquaint yourself with any of the techniques that are new to you before you ask your students to undertake the project.
>
> . . . Decide on your project and assemble the materials before you begin.
>
> . . . Make a sample model for experience.
>
> . . . Use a flat surface for working.
>
> . . . Be sure the paper is cut exactly to measurements and that folds are straight.
>
> . . . Be available for consultation.
>
> . . . Provide guidance on what the next logical step is to encourage all students to finish their projects.
>
> . . . Use the finished craft projects as displays and points of interest for your school's open house.

• Many of the Incentive Badges found in each Unit are open-ended and can be made effective communication tools to meet your needs. Extra space is provided on these badges for additional written messages that might be used for any number of reasons. Be creative for your own special needs; load the copier with colored paper and print as many as you need for the semester or entire school year. Then simply use a paper cutter to separate the badges and sort them out alphabetically. Make an alphabetical index on file card dividers using these titles. Next, arrange them in an accessible file box or shoe box, depending on the size needed. Include a roll of tape to attach the badge to the recipient.

Teacher's Guide to Unit 4

Musical Instruments and the Voice is a collection of 50 activities that provides valuable lessons for learning the characteristics of and understanding musical instruments and the human voice. The activities include classifying, matching, listing, researching, naming, decoding, and identifying.

Unit 4 is divided into nine parts to make the teaching of instruments easy and enjoyable. The first, "Self-Assessment," will help you discover much about your students' interests, background, and prior knowledge of various musical instruments. Encourage students to do original artwork for the creative drawing activities in this and other sections of this unit.

The second section, "Library Research," is designed for a small group of students within the classroom, or for individual students doing independent study. A quick look at the particular activity sheets will tell you if the lesson lends itself to a classroom situation or whether special resource information is needed.

"Band, Orchestral, and Folk Instruments" is a broad collection of activities to provide useful information about these various instruments. The "Word List" at the back of this unit will be a handy tool for students to check proper spelling. In this part, and throughout the unit, the illustrations resemble the actual instruments as closely as possible. However, the instruments are not drawn in proportion with one another.

The next five sections each deal with specific families of the orchestra. Do not feel that you have to cover all the activities in each part. It is better to introduce less material and teach it well.

The activity sheets end with a section on learning about the voice, which introduces facts about the voice. Take the opportunity to correlate what is learned in the activities with actual singing experiences in the classroom.

The activities in Unit 4 may be sequenced in a variety of ways. While studying traditional instruments, the class could simply learn about one family of instruments and, when finished, continue on to the next. The class could also be divided into small groups, each learning about a different family of instruments and reporting its findings to the class.

Contents

Activity Number/Title	Skill Involved	Level of Difficulty
Self-Assessment		
4-1 SEE MY CUBBY!	Drawing a favorite instrument	Beginner
4-2 DREAMING	Drawing an instrument of the future	Beginner
4-3 DO I FIT THE INSTRUMENT?	Naming an instrument by reading the requirements to play it	Beginner
4-4 DO I QUALIFY?	Naming an instrument by reading the requirements to play it	Beginner
Library Research		
4-5 LIST THE BOOKS	Listing and classifying books on instruments of the orchestra	Beginner
4-6 CHART THE INFORMATION	Researching various musical instruments	Beginner
4-7 NOW AND THEN	Matching old-fashioned instruments with ones currently in use	Beginner
Band, Orchestral, and Folk Instruments		
4-8 SEAT THE ORCHESTRA	Completing a seating chart for the modern symphony orchestra	Beginner
4-9 TUNING UP THE ORCHESTRA	Reading for comprehension on how the orchestra tunes	Beginner
4-10 PICTURE PUZZLE #1	Naming instruments from picture clues	Beginner
4-11 PICTURE PUZZLE #2	Naming instruments from picture clues	Beginner
4-12 PICTURE PUZZLE #3	Naming instruments from picture clues	Beginner

Contents

Activity Number/Title	Skill Involved	Level of Difficulty
4–48 NUMBER THEIR MUSIC	Matching voice type with the description	Intermediate
4–49 WHAT'S THE RANGE?	Writing voice type and matching with its range in pitch	Intermediate
4–50 DISTRIBUTE THEIR MUSIC	Matching singers to pitch range on vocal scores	Advanced

Activities for ASSESSMENT

1

SEE MY CUBBY!   4–1

Here is a picture of your cubby. In it draw your favorite instrument, or one you'd like to learn to play.

(Write your name here.)

Name _____

Score _____

Date _____

Class _____

DREAMING

4–2

It's rest time. Draw a picture of yourself with your head on the pillow. Then draw a picture of yourself playing an instrument of the future.

Name _____

Date _____

Score _____

Class _____

DO I FIT THE INSTRUMENT?

4–3

Before reading the directions, fold your paper back on the dotted line.

A musician needs certain qualifications to play some musical instruments. Before selecting an instrument to play, it is good to know what abilities and characteristics are required. Read the statements below and write the name of the instrument on the blank that fits the requirement. For each answer, write the letters directly above the numbers. When you are finished, check your answers with the number code at the bottom of the page.

1. You need a sharp ear to match the exact pitch on the strings and to hear the tone quality while bowing. You also need to be agile from the fingers on up to the shoulders.

   _____
   5   18   12   15   18   13

2. The performer needs a keen ear to tune its 43 strings.

   _____
   19   26   9   11

3. The performer must have the ability to direct a small stream of air across a hole on the mouthpiece of this instrument.

   _____
   21   15   6   7   22

4. This percussion instrument requires a good sense of rhythm along with hand coordination.

   _____
   8   13   26   9   22   23   9   6   14

5. The ability to coordinate fingers, hands, and arms with the distance between the keyboard and the music are needed with this instrument.

   _____
   11   18   26   13   12

. . . . fold back here . . . .

A	B	C	D	E	F	G	H	I	J	K	L	M
26	25	24	23	22	21	20	19	18	17	16	15	14

N	O	P	Q	R	S	T	U	V	W	X	Y	Z
13	12	11	10	9	8	7	6	5	4	3	2	1

Name _____

Date _____

Score _____

Class _____

DO I QUALIFY?

Before reading the directions, fold your paper back on the dotted line.

When selecting an instrument to play, it is good to know what abilities or characteristics are required. Read the statements below and write the name of the instrument on the blank that fits the requirement. For each answer, write the letters directly above the numbers. When you are finished, check your answers with the number code at the bottom of the page.

1. You must have an alert ear to help move the slide to the exact position.

   _____
   7   19   12   14   25   12   13   22

2. Hand and foot coordination is needed when playing the keyboards and pedals on this instrument.

   _____
   12   9   20   26   13

3. You need large enough hands and fingers to cover the keys and holes of this woodwind instrument.

   _____
   8   26   3   12   11   19   12   13   22

4. Lip control and nimble fingers are called for when learning to play this double reed instrument.

   _____
   12   25   12   22

5. You must have a quick, alert ear to change chords while playing a song with this instrument.

   _____
   20   6   18   7   26   9

. . . . fold back here . . . .

A	B	C	D	E	F	G	H	I	J	K	L	M
26	25	24	23	22	21	20	19	18	17	16	15	14

N	O	P	Q	R	S	T	U	V	W	X	Y	Z
13	12	11	10	9	8	7	6	5	4	3	2	1

Activities for
LIBRARY RESEARCH

LIST THE BOOKS   4-5

Make a list of books about instruments of the orchestra. Use your school library. Include the title, author, publisher, and call number.

TITLE	AUTHOR	PUBLISHER	CALL NUMBER

Name _____   Score _____

Date _____   Class _____

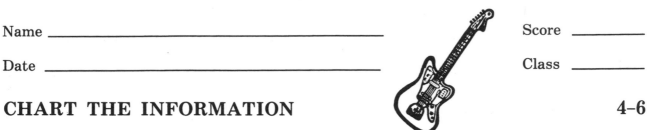

CHART THE INFORMATION

4–6

Research the following instruments. Then complete the chart.

Name of Instrument	What clef is used?	Describe the Instrument	Name an Instrumentalist
PIANO			
GUITAR			
CLARINET			
OTHER: _____ _____			

NOW AND THEN

Here are eight different instruments. Draw a line connecting the old-fashioned instrument to the current model. Circle the instruments that are used today.

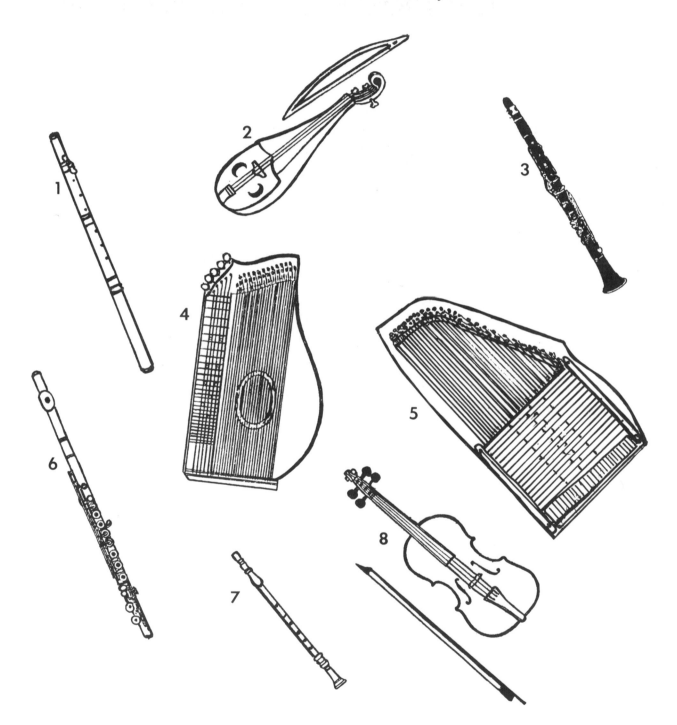

Activities for Learning About
BAND, ORCHESTRAL, AND FOLK INSTRUMENTS

SEAT THE ORCHESTRA

This is a standard seating plan for the modern symphony orchestra. Show where each group of instruments belongs. Write the names in the correct sections.

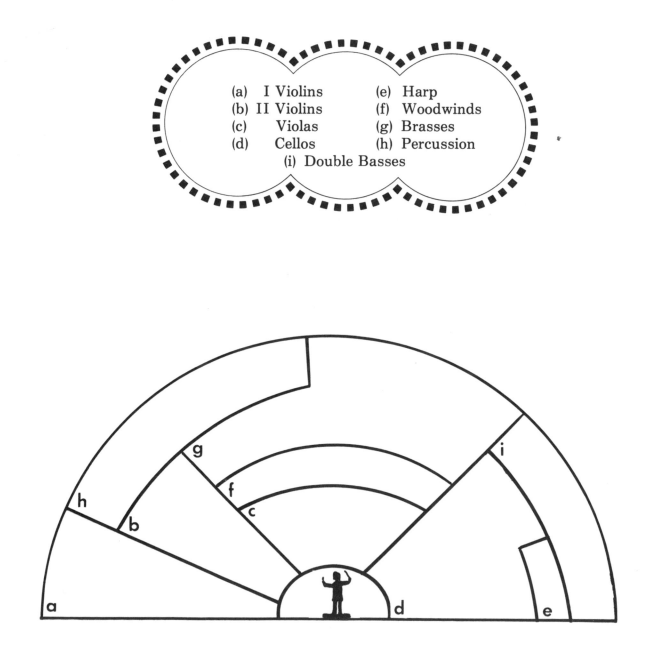

(a) I Violins   (e) Harp
(b) II Violins   (f) Woodwinds
(c) Violas   (g) Brasses
(d) Cellos   (h) Percussion
(i) Double Basses

Name _____

Date _____

Score _____

Class _____

TUNING UP THE ORCHESTRA

Read the story and underline all of the music terms. Then find twelve of the music terms in the word search and circle them. The words can be found horizontally, vertically, and diagonally. HINT: The words to look for are found at the bottom of the sheet.

If you were backstage in a concert hall before the concert began, you would see all the musicians warming up and tuning their instruments. There are four different families of instruments represented in the symphony orchestra. They are the strings, woodwinds, brass, and percussion. The strings are the most important family of the symphony orchestra. When the orchestra members are seated on stage, the first violinist will enter and walk to the front, face the orchestra, and bow. The audience honors the first violinist, called the "concert master" by applauding. This is the first indication that the concert is about to begin. After the applause stops, the orchestra tunes to the concert "A" played by the first chair oboist. The members of the orchestra will adjust their instruments to match the exact pitch as they tune up. After the symphony members have the best intonation possible, the conductor will enter and the concert will begin.

```
P O S I L D A E M N O R C W P X E U P M A
G H M Y Z C O N C E R T M A S T E R M U V
I Q E B M B R U M K M T O R T L K J I T A
P M U A D P C X U T I N S T R U M E N T S
I T G S U D H J M D E A M L I W Z Y M E T
T J U S V W E O E Y I N T O N A T I O N E
C E N N E R S U N I Q X T G G M W U X Y P
H I N N E D T M A Y P Y N W S X I A N E O
D I W A E R X Y C N C O N C E R T Q E D
M C E I O D A W O O D W I N D Z Y I E Y S
```

ORCHESTRA   INTONATION   TUNES
SYMPHONY   CONCERT MASTER   WOODWIND
PITCH   INSTRUMENTS   BASS
TUNE   STRINGS   CONCERT

PICTURE PUZZLE #1   4–10

Write the name of each instrument in the puzzle.

ACROSS

1.

4.

6.

7.

8.

DOWN

2.

3.

5.

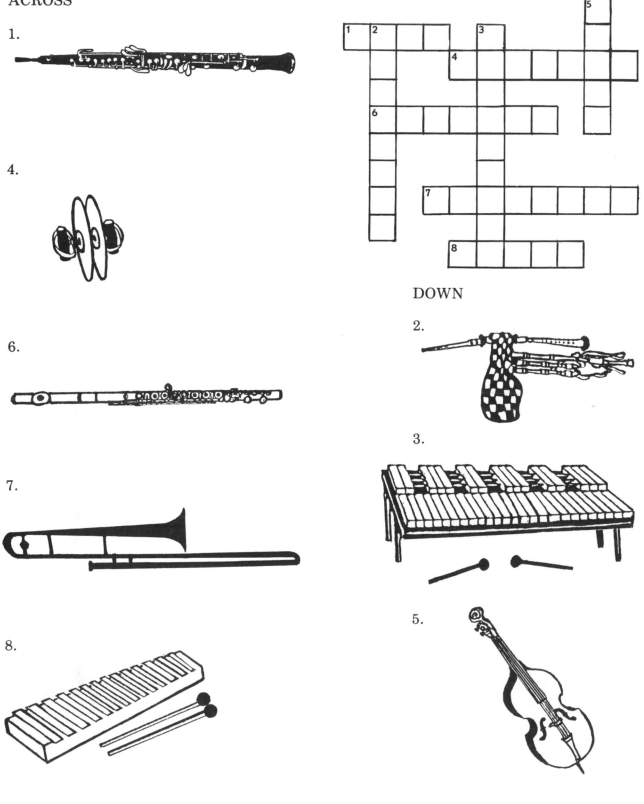

Name _____   Score _____

Date _____   Class _____

PICTURE PUZZLE #2   4–11

Write the name of each instrument in the puzzle.

ACROSS   DOWN

3.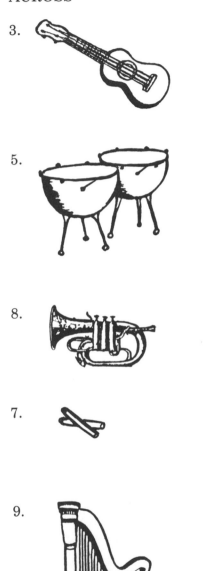

1.

5.

8.

7.

9.

PICTURE PUZZLE #3

Write the name of each instrument in the puzzle.

DOWN

1.

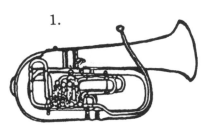

2.

3.

5.

6.

ACROSS

4.

5.

6.

7. _____ organ

8.

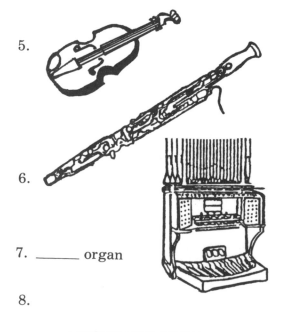

THE MISSING PART   4–13

Circle the instrument that needs the missing part.

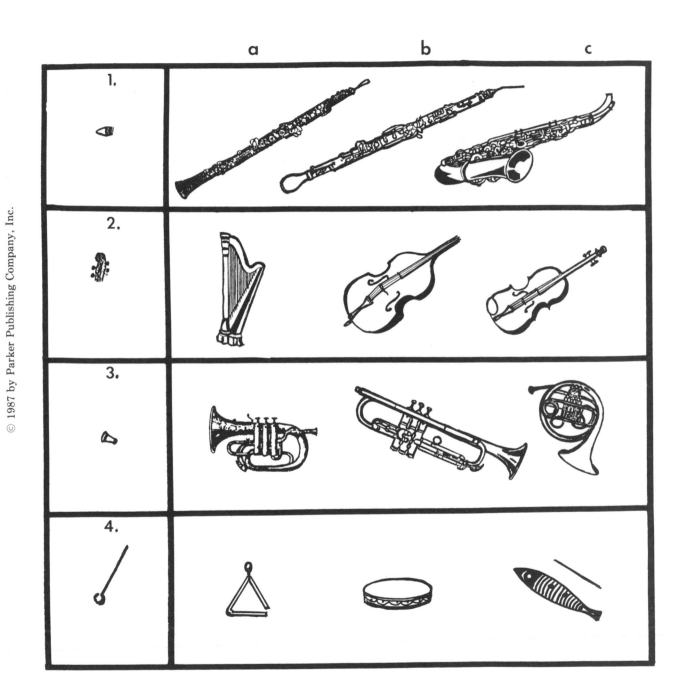

Name _____   Score _____

Date _____   Class _____

WHAT'S MISSING?   4–14

Part of each instrument is missing. Draw the missing part and write the name of the instrument by the number.

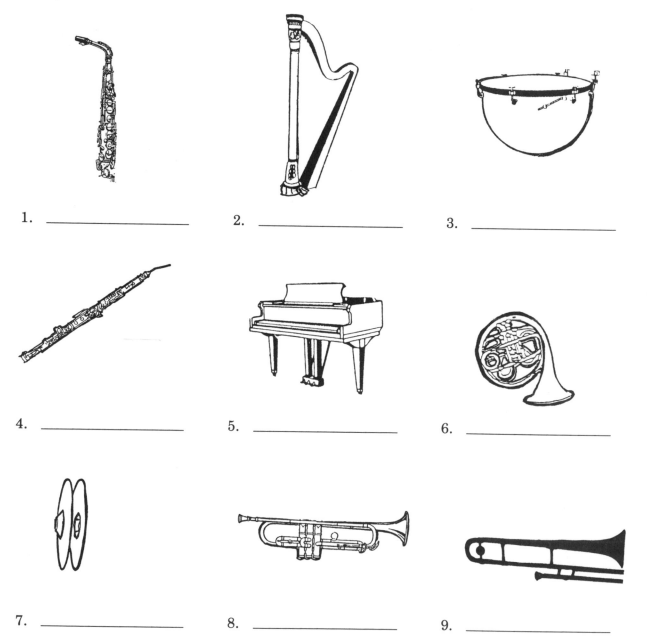

1. _____   2. _____   3. _____

4. _____   5. _____   6. _____

7. _____   8. _____   9. _____

Name _____   Score _____

Date _____   Class _____

WHAT'S THE MISSING SYLLABLE?   4–15

Complete the following two-syllable instrument names. The pictures provide the clues for the missing syllables.

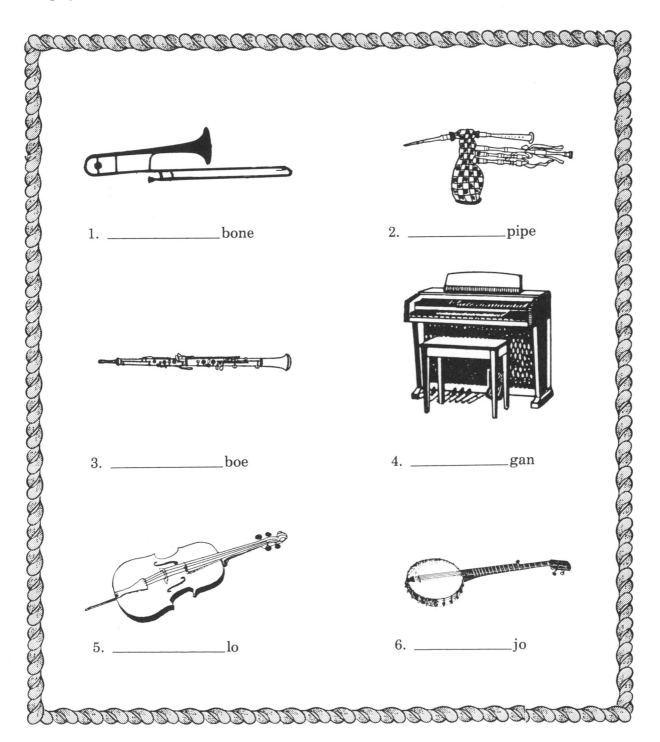

1. _____bone   2. _____pipe

3. _____boe   4. _____gan

5. _____lo   6. _____jo

FIND THE MEMBERS

4–16

Circle the matching family members.

	a.	b.	c.	d.	e.
1. PERCUSSION					
2. STRING					
3. KEYBOARD					
4. BRASS					
5. WOODWIND					

BRING IT ALONG   4–17

In the suitcase are several items belonging to the instruments below. Draw the item by the instrument. Then write the name of the instrument under the picture.

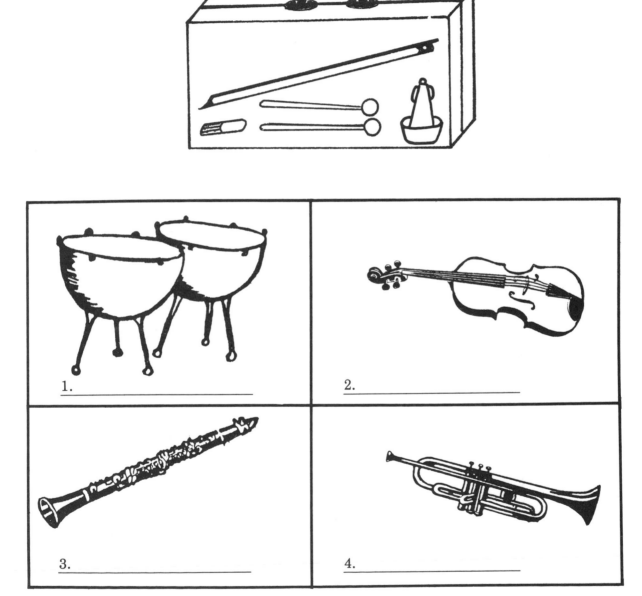

1. _____   2. _____

3. _____   4. _____

Now put the correct number of stars after each: Brass Family   *
Woodwind Family **
String Family   ***
Percussion Family ****

WHAT'S IN COMMON?   4–18

Each set of the following three instruments has something in common. Choose your answer from the bottom of the page and write it on the blank.

1. _____   piccolo
                                          violin
                                          trumpet

2. _____   contrabassoon
                                          tuba
                                          double bass

3. _____   trumpet
                                          French horn
                                          trombone

4. _____   clarinet
                                          saxophone
                                          bass clarinet

5. _____   oboe
                                          bassoon
                                          contrabassoon

6. _____   xylophone
                                          glockenspiel
                                          chimes

7. _____   tambourine
                                          maracas
                                          jingle bells

8. _____   harp
                                          viola
                                          cello

Answers in mixed order:

a. strings
b. strike with mallet — percussion
c. double reed — woodwind
d. lowest pitched in orchestra
e. highest pitched in orchestra
f. single reed — woodwind
g. brass
h. shake — percussion

Name _____

Date _____

Score _____

Class _____

NAME THREE

4–19

Name three instruments that have the following in common:

1. Uses a bow   _____   _____   _____

2. Has a double reed   _____   _____   _____

3. Has a single reed   _____   _____   _____

4. Uses a mute   _____   _____   _____

5. Should stand up to play   _____   _____   _____

6. You must sit down to play   _____   _____   _____

7. Has strings   _____   _____   _____

8. Is made of brass   _____   _____   _____

9. Made of stretched skin   _____   _____   _____

10. Uses mallets   _____   _____   _____

11. Has a keyboard   _____   _____   _____

12. Has a bridge   _____   _____   _____

13. Uses a plectrum or pick   _____   _____   _____

14. Uses a foot pedal   _____   _____   _____

15. Hit with a stick or beater   _____   _____   _____

16. Strike one part against the other   _____   _____   _____

17. Unpitched   _____   _____   _____

18. Electronic or mechanical   _____   _____   _____

WHAT'S THE DIFFERENCE?   4–20

Name the following eight instruments. Then explain how, in each set, one instrument is different from the other.

EXPLANATION

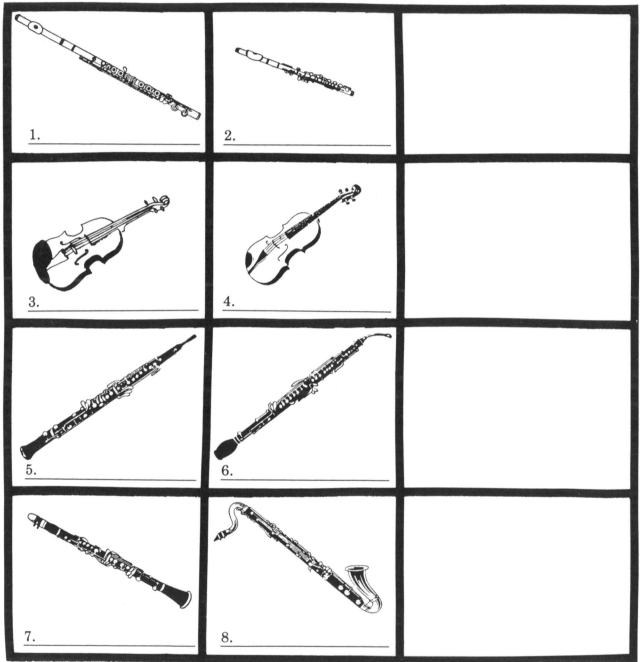

1. _____

2. _____

3. _____

4. _____

5. _____

6. _____

7. _____

8. _____

MAKE UP YOUR MIND   4-21

Decide if these instruments are played by either standing or sitting. Under the name write an "O" if you would usually stand or an "X" if you would usually sit to play the instrument.

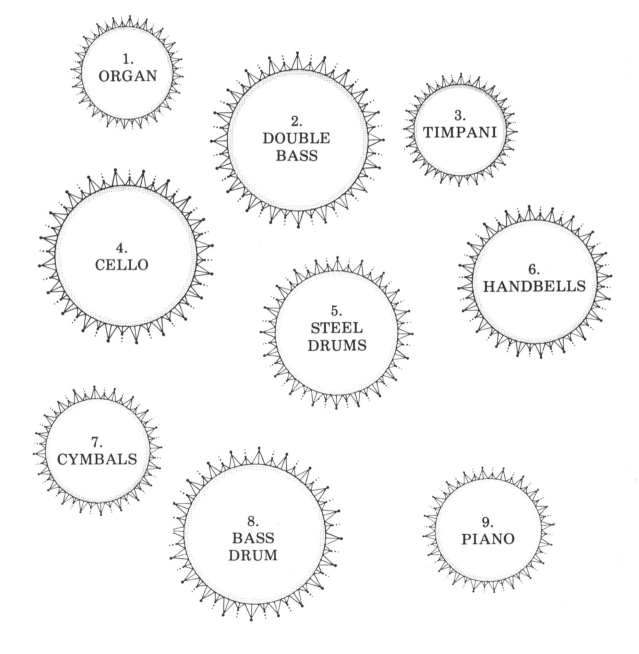

CHOOSE THE MUSIC   4–22

Imagine that you are an instrument teacher. Five of your students need music for a solo. Match each instrument with its range in pitch by writing the letter of the instrument in the box by the staff.

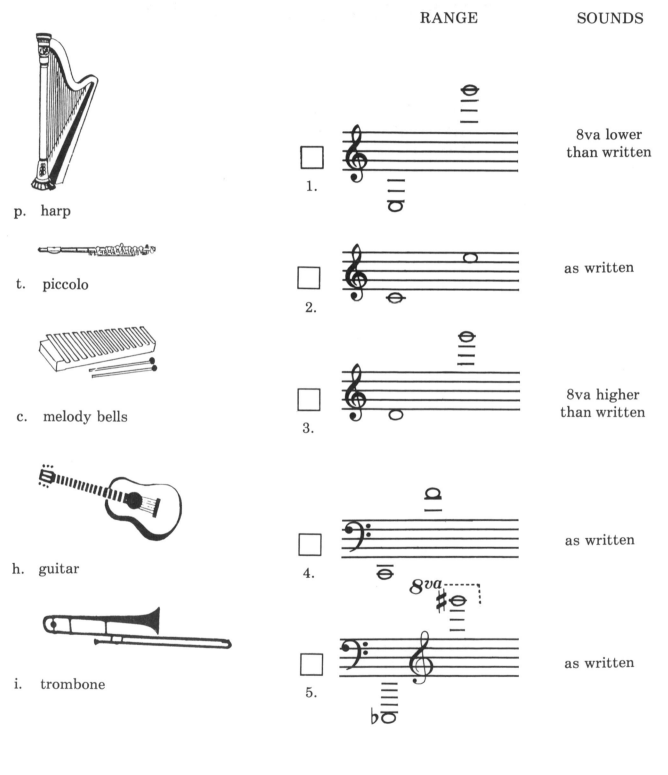

p. harp

t. piccolo

c. melody bells

h. guitar

i. trombone

RANGE   SOUNDS

1.   8va lower
                         than written

2.   as written

3.   8va higher
                         than written

4.   as written

5.   as written

Activities for
GETTING TO KNOW THE BRASS

Name _____   Score _____

Date _____   Class _____

HELP DETECTIVE BRASSO   4–23

Help Detective Brasso solve his case by unscrambling the mystery word. First write the word that fits at the end of each sentence below. Then unscramble the circled letters to spell the mystery word.

1. The number of valves on a trumpet __ __ (__) __ __

2. An instrument having a slide __ __ __ __ __ (__) __ __

3. A pear-shaped metal or wood object inserted into the bell __ __ (__) __

4. The highest sounding brass instrument __ (__) __ __ __ __ __

5. A military instrument __ __ __ __ (__)

6. Another name for the French Horn (__) __ __ __

7. The lowest pitched brass instrument __ __ __ (__)

8. A type of trombone __ __ (__) __

9. An instrument similar to the trumpet (__) __ __ __ __ __

Mystery word: __ __ __ __ __ __ __ __ __

NOTE THE BRASS   4–24

The names of these instruments all have missing letters. Use the notes above the words to write the matching letters on the blanks. Then write the name that belongs to each instrument below.

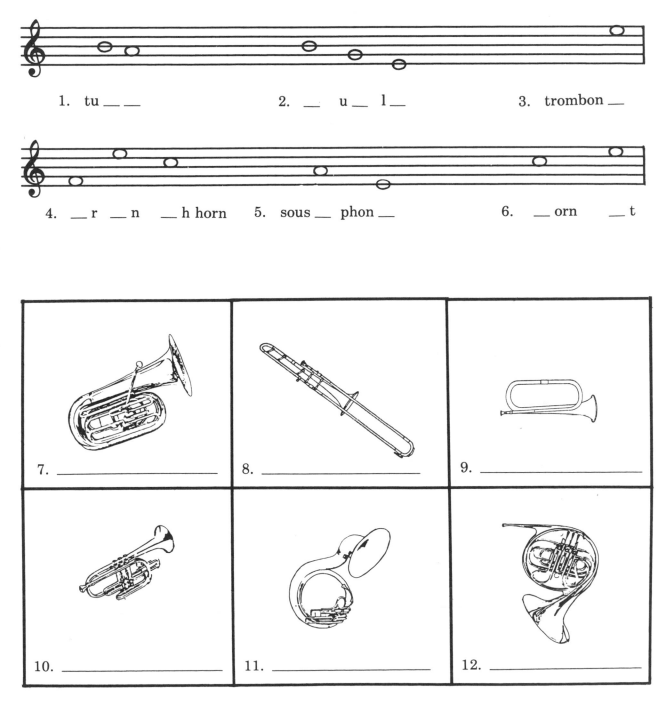

1. tu __ __   2. __ u __ l __   3. trombon __

4. __ r __ n __ h horn   5. sous __ phon __   6. __ orn __ t

7. _____   8. _____   9. _____

10. _____   11. _____   12. _____

BRASS FACTS   4-25

Read each sentence. Circle the letter under "Yes" if it tells something true about the instrument. Circle the letter under "No" if it tells something that is not true.

		Yes	No
1.	Trombone means "big trumpet."	D	T
2.	The trombone has three valves.	A	I
3.	The trombone is made of four brass tubes.	S	K
4.	On the trombone, pitch is varied by sliding one tube in and out of the other.	T	S
5.	The French Horn is the smallest brass instrument.	E	R
6.	The French Horn is used in the orchestra	A	U
7.	The French horn is commonly known as the "horn."	M	G
8.	The French horn is made of 200 feet of tubing circled around to shape the instrument.	T	S
9.	Besides the use of the lips and valves to change pitch, the player uses his hand to vary the pitch and tone by placing it in the bell of the instrument.	Y	O
10.	The tuba is the largest of the brass instruments and plays the highest tones.	N	R
11.	We often raise or lower the flag to the sound of the bugle.	E	O
12.	Only the pressure of the player's lips and the force of the player's breath will change the pitch of the trumpet.	D	V

Activities for
GETTING TO KNOW THE KEYBOARD

PIANO CARE QUIZ

Read each sentence. Fill in the blanks using a letter name of a key from the piano.

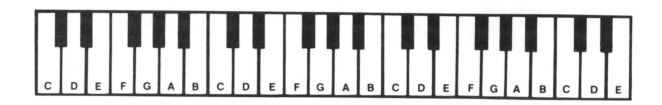

1. The type of pedal used to sust __ in a sound is called a damper.

2. The strings in a grand piano are horizont __ l.

3. One of the best ways of caring for a piano is to play it r __ __ ul __ rly.

4. One of the worst enemies of the piano is __ __ mpn __ ss, because it will rust the strings.

5. Another h __ rmful thing to a piano is dry heat.

6. The proper humi __ ity for a room with a piano should be between fifty and sixty-five percent.

7. If the humidity is too low it is recommended that you install a humi __ i __ i __ r.

8. Contrary to popular opinion, it is better not to close the cover of the piano after you've finished pl __ yin __ it.

9. By keeping the cover __ los __ __ you may encourage moths.

10. When a piano is moved from one place to another, the pitch will likely change, and the piano will need to be r __ tun __ __.

11. If the piano keys are ivory, they may be __ l __ __ n __ __ by wiping them with a damp soapy cloth.

12. Do not use furniture polish on a pi __ no's finish.

Name _____   Score _____

Date _____   Class _____

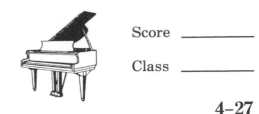

THE PIANO PUZZLE

4–27

Complete the missing words in the sentences. Then rewrite the letters from each word at the bottom of the page to match the numbers. When you have filled in the letters correctly, the letters will spell out one more statement about the piano. (Some letters will be used with more than one number.)

1. The black and white __ __ __ __ on the piano form a definite __ __ __ __ __ __ __.
   9 45 11 37   30 6 34 41 22 43 20

2. At the extreme left on the __ __ __ __ __ __ __ __ the pitch will be the lowest.
   8 10 11 4 28 38 18 40

3. On the piano, the __ __ __ __ __ __ and thicker the strings, the lower the pitch.
   5 36 39 26 44 27

4. Piano music is written on two sets of staffs. The treble clef sign on the upper staff

   __ __ __ __ __ __ __ __ __ music played by the right __ __ __ __.
   24 25 23 24 7 13 1 3 31   42 16 39 23

5. The __ __ __ __ __ staff for piano music uses the __ __ __ __ clef and is usually played with
   5 32 35 45 14   4 19 46 12

   the __ __ __ __ hand.
   5 15 33 41

6. When looking at an easy piano piece, the numbers by the notes are for

   __ __ __ __ __ __ __ __ __, making it __ __ __ __ __ __ __ for the beginning performer.
   33 24 39 21 44 17 24 20 26   2 15 5 30 33 29 5

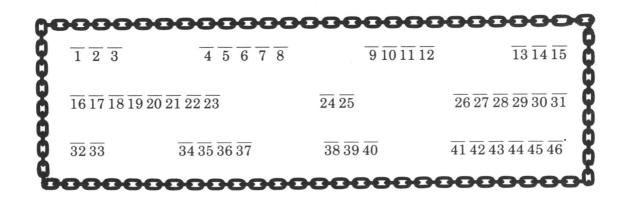

A SYNTHESIZER STICKLER   4–28

Finish these sentences by selecting your answers from the list at the bottom of the sheet.

1. Synthesizers recreate _____

   _____.

2. In a synthesizer all sound waves _____.

3. The higher the pitch, _____.

4. The use of filters adds or eliminates _____.

5. The four stages of a sound are _____

   _____.

6. Attack, decay, sustain, and release are regulated by the envelope generator and are known

   as _____.

7. A sequencer is a storage unit that _____

   _____.

8. The polyphonic synthesizer produces _____.

9. Electronic music may be referred to as _____.

10. Digital synthesizers produce sounds completely _____.

can memorize an entire musical line
by computer
harmonic frequencies in order to shape the sound
pitch, tone, volume, and articulation all electronically
ADSR
are produced by an oscillator
synthetic music
attack, sustain, decay, and release
the more frequently the sound wave vibrates
more than one note at a time

Activities for
GETTING TO KNOW THE PERCUSSION

MAKE YOUR OWN

4-29

Pretend you are an authority on percussion instruments and you have been asked by a preschool teacher to instruct the children in making some rhythm instruments. Use the format below to design three more instruments that can make a sound by ringing, tapping, tinkling, rattling, or booming. Make sure the instruments are durable, safe, and have a pleasant sound.

TYPE OF SOUND: tinkling

NAME OF INSTRUMENT:
          Jingle stick

MATERIALS: 4 jingle bells, cord, tongue
     depressor

PROCEDURE: Drill holes in tongue
     depressor. Fasten bells to wood with
     the cord.

ILLUSTRATION:

TYPE OF SOUND:

NAME OF INSTRUMENT:

MATERIALS:

PROCEDURE:

ILLUSTRATION:

TYPE OF SOUND:

NAME OF INSTRUMENT:

MATERIALS:

PROCEDURE

ILLUSTRATION:

TYPE OF SOUND:

TYPE OF INSTRUMENT:

MATERIALS:

PROCEDURE:

ILLUSTRATION:

Name _____   Score _____

Date _____   Class _____

CREATE A RHYTHM SCORE   4–30

Use these instruments to compose a rhythm score. Line one is done to show you how.

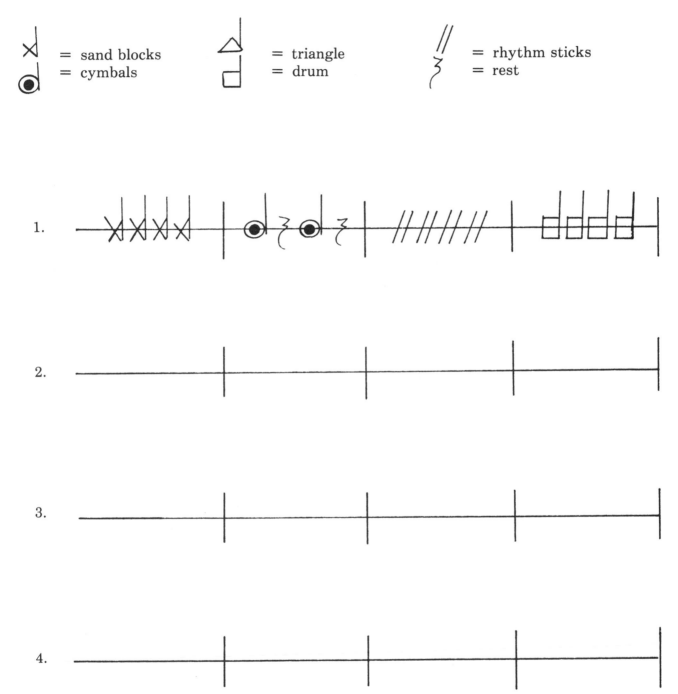

X = sand blocks

● = cymbals

△ = triangle

▭ = drum

// = rhythm sticks

⌇ = rest

1.

2.

3.

4.

DECODE THE PERCUSSION INSTRUMENTS 4–31

Use this code to identify these popular classroom percussion instruments.

A	B	C	D	E	F	G	H	I	J	K	L	M
1	2	3	4	5	6	7	8	9	10	11	12	13

N	O	P	Q	R	S	T	U	V	W	X	Y	Z
14	15	16	17	18	19	20	21	22	23	24	25	26

1. Blocks covered with sandpaper and rubbed together are called

   $\overline{19}\ \overline{1}\ \overline{14}\ \overline{4}\quad \overline{1}\ \overline{12}\ \overline{15}\ \overline{3}\ \overline{11}\ \overline{19}$

2. This instrument can be shaken or hit with a drumstick.

   $\overline{3}\ \overline{15}\ \overline{23}\ \overline{2}\ \overline{5}\ \overline{12}\ \overline{12}$

3. Use a hard mallet to strike this instrument just above the slit of this rectangular block of hardwood.

   $\overline{23}\ \overline{15}\ \overline{15}\ \overline{4}\quad \overline{2}\ \overline{12}\ \overline{15}\ \overline{3}\ \overline{11}$

4. This instrument is made from the castana (chestnut) tree and is the traditional instrument of the Spanish folk dancer.

   $\overline{3}\ \overline{1}\ \overline{19}\ \overline{20}\ \overline{1}\ \overline{14}\ \overline{5}\ \overline{20}\ \overline{19}$

5. A skin covers this round hoop with pairs of jingles.

   $\overline{20}\ \overline{1}\ \overline{13}\ \overline{2}\ \overline{15}\ \overline{21}\ \overline{18}\ \overline{9}\ \overline{14}\ \overline{5}$

6. The open corner of this triangular shaped instrument prevents the sound from being any particular pitch. It's made with a small round bar of steel suspended with a loop of cord. A metal beater strikes the instrument to produce a clear "tingling" sound.

   $\overline{20}\ \overline{18}\ \overline{9}\ \overline{1}\ \overline{14}\ \overline{7}\ \overline{12}\ \overline{5}$

7. When the player crashes these two metal discs together it usually indicates a climax in the music.

   $\overline{3}\ \overline{25}\ \overline{13}\ \overline{2}\ \overline{1}\ \overline{12}\ \overline{19}$

STRICTLY STRIKERS AND SHAKERS   4–32

The pictures of strikers and shakers are shown below. Write the missing letters of their names in the boxes of the Word Puzzle.

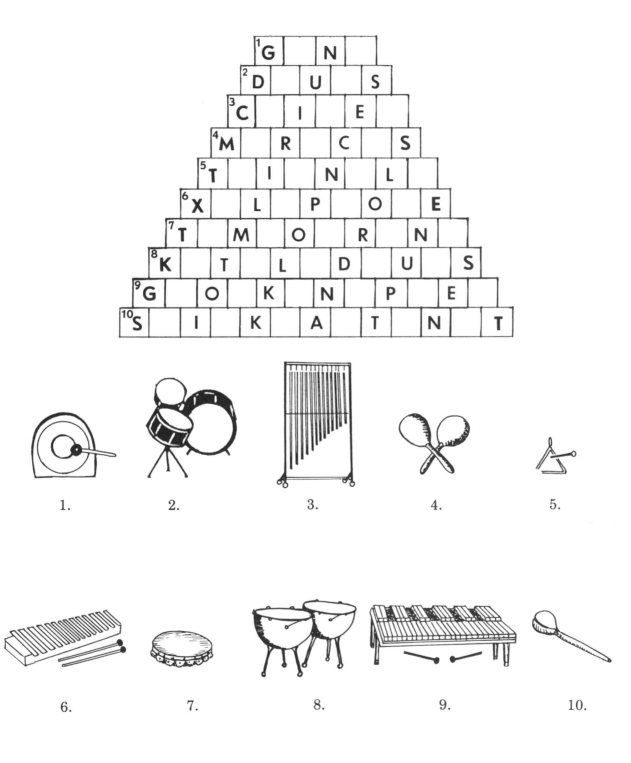

1. 2. 3. 4. 5.

6. 7. 8. 9. 10.

SHENANIGANS

The music monkey has been playing some shenanigans again. He mixed the percussion instruments and put some in the wrong boxes. Sort out the boxes by circling each instrument that is in the right box.

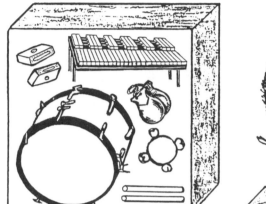

1. BOOMING

3. TAPPING

2. RINGING

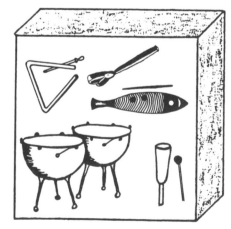

4. TINKLING

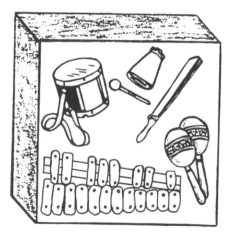

5. RATTLING

Name _____   Score _____

Date _____   Class _____

PERCUSSION FACTS   4–34

Read each sentence. Circle "Yes" if it tells something true about the instrument. Circle "No" if it tells something that is not true.

1.	Bass drums are all the same size.	YES	NO
2.	The beaters used on the snare drum to produce various rhythmic patterns are usually made of lamb's wool.	YES	NO
3.	The pedals at the base of the timpani are used to tighten or loosen the skin, changing the pitch.	YES	NO
4.	Another name for the timpani is "steel drums."	YES	NO
5.	Percussion instruments that produce tones by striking or shaking are the wood block, triangle, maracas, tambourine, cymbals, castanets, and the gong.	YES	NO
6.	There are members of the percussion family that produce definite pitches.	YES	NO
7.	When you hear a loud, crashing sound in a band or orchestra, it is probably the sound of the tambourine.	YES	NO
8.	Gypsy music makes use of the gong and chimes.	YES	NO
9.	The guiro is a gourd that has ridges cut in it to be played by running a scraper back and forth over the notches.	YES	NO
10.	The xylophone and marimba are usually made of wood.	YES	NO
11.	Castanets are gourds with peas or beans inside designed for shaking.	YES	NO
12.	Mallets are used to play the glockenspiel.	YES	NO

Activities for
GETTING TO KNOW THE STRINGS

A STRING OF MULTIPLE CHOICES   4-35

This is a test of your knowledge of stringed instruments. The questions are followed by three answers. Choose the answer you think is correct and write the letter on the line in front of each question.

_____ 1. Sound is produced on a string when it

    h. hums   i. vibrates   j. acoustics

_____ 2. If a loose, thick string makes a lower sound, what will a thin, tight string make?

    l. a deeper sound   m. a wider sound   n. a higher sound

_____ 3. What two instruments are held beneath the chin?

    s. cello and double bass   t. viola and violin   u. violin and harp

_____ 4. Bows are usually made from pernambuco wood and

    e. nylon or horsehair   f. arrows or plectrums   g. string or rosin

_____ 5. What is the device used to tighten and loosen the bow?

    k. a turtle   l. a frog   m. a screwdriver

_____ 6. Why is a mute used on a violin?

    l. to muffle the sound   m. to stop the sound   n. to vibrate the sound

_____ 7. To produce a tone on a stringed instrument one can either draw a bow across the strings or

    g. adjust the strings   h. tap the soundboard   i. pluck the strings

_____ 8. What is the most important section of the orchestra?

    g. string   h. woodwind   i. brass

_____ 9. What is the most important instrument in the orchestra?

    d. trumpet   e. violin   f. double bass

_____ 10. What should be put on a bow before each practice session?

    m. a frog   n. rosin   o. fingerboard

_____ 11. What do these instruments have in common: guitar, banjo, ukulele, mandolin, sitar, autoharp, harp?

    s. they all have scrolls   t. they are not played with a bow

          u. they do not have a bridge

Name _____   Score _____

Date _____   Class _____

GETTING INTO THE STRING OF THINGS   4–36

One word in each of these sentences about stringed instruments is missing all of the letters except for the "o's." Finish the sentences by writing the missing letters on the blanks.

1. When a string vibrates it produces a _ o _ _ _ .

2. A thin, tight string makes a higher sound than a thick _ o o _ _ string.

3. There are _ o _ _ strings on the violin, viola, cello, and double bass.

4. Two instruments held under the chin are the violin and _ _ o _ _ .

5. All the members of the violin family are played with a _ o _ .

6. Bows are usually made from pernambuco wood and nylon or _ o _ _ _ hair.

7. The hair on the bow is tightened with the _ _ o _ .

8. Rosin should be put on the _ o _ every time it is used.

9. A mute is used to muffle the sound of a _ o _ _ _ instrument.

10. There are _ _ o violin sections in an orchestra.

11. A sound can be produced by either plucking the string or drawing a bow _ _ _ o _ _ the string.

12. The most important instrument in the orchestra is the _ _ o _ _ _ .

13. The performer must be seated to play the _ _ _ _ o .

14. The strings of the cello sound an o _ _ _ _ _ lower than those of the viola.

GUITAR GRAMMAR

4–37

At the right are a list of words related to the guitar. Write the words on the blanks to match the various parts of the guitar. Then study the diagram of the keyboard and staff to write in the letter names of the strings.

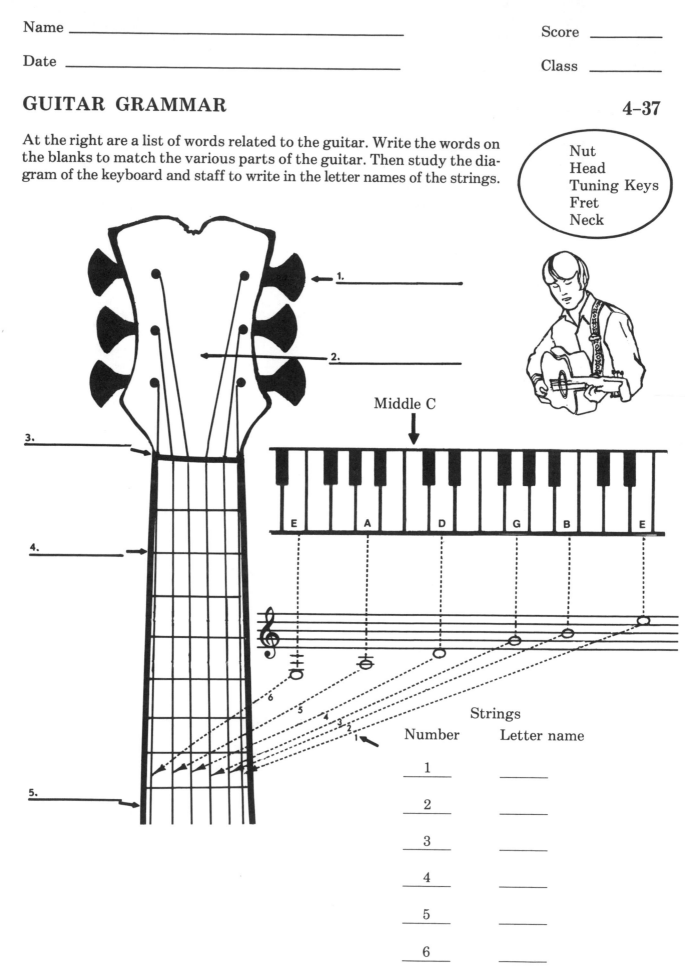

Nut
Head
Tuning Keys
Fret
Neck

Middle C

Strings	
Number	Letter name
1	____
2	____
3	____
4	____
5	____
6	____

STRING FACTS   4-38

Read each sentence. Circle the letter under "Yes" if it tells something true about the instrument. Circle the letter under "No" if it tells something that is not true.

		Yes	*No*
1.	The string family consists mainly of five instruments: the violin, viola, cello, double bass, and harp.	F	P
2.	The double bass usually plays the melody line.	O	I
3.	One of the special effects created by the use of the bow is when two or more notes are played at once, called double stopping.	N	I
4.	The technique of plucking the strings, called pizzicato, can only be done on the violin.	R	E
5.	Antonio Stradivarius is known as a great violin maker.	A	S
6.	There are forty-three pedals at the base of the harp used to raise or lower the pitch of the strings.	O	N
7.	The violin is a seventh larger in size than the viola.	L	D
8.	The viola is the soprano of the string family.	U	D
9.	The strings of the cello are one octave higher than those of the viola.	T	A
10.	The harp was used in Biblical times.	N	I
11.	The strings on the cello are thicker than those on the double bass.	O	D
12.	The cello is also referred to as the violoncello.	Y	N

MATCH THE PARTS WITH THEIR NAMES   4–39

Listed below are the names of parts for the violin, viola, cello, bass, and the bow. On each blank, write the matching letter for the part. When you finish, your answers reading down will spell the part of a stringed instrument.

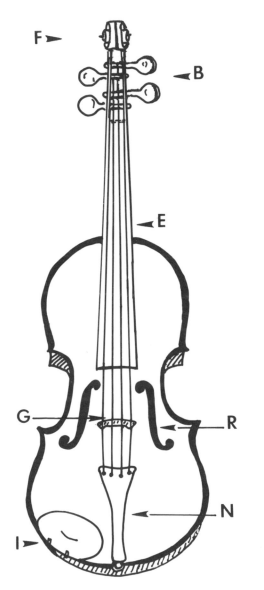

INSTRUMENT

1. ____ Scroll

2. ____ Chin rest

3. ____ Tailpiece (string holder)

4. ____ Bridge

5. ____ Neck

6. ____ F holes (sound holes)

7. ____ Pegs

8. ____ End pin for cello and bass

BOW

9. ____ Hair

10. ____ Frog

11. ____ Point or tip of bow

Write your answers in order here:

— — — — — — — — — — —

IT'S TUNE-UP TIME   4–40

Write the names of the instruments on the blanks.

The following staffs show the open strings of the instruments. Decide which belongs to which by writing the matching letter of the instrument in the block.

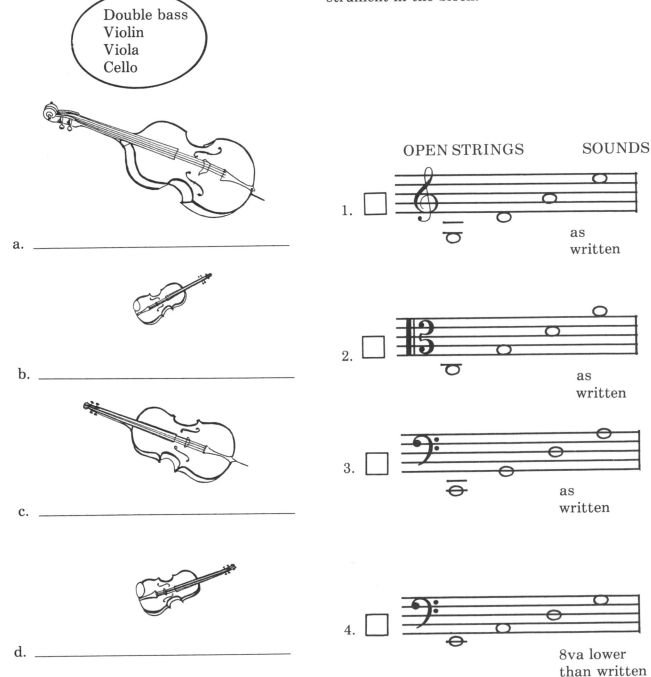

Double bass
Violin
Viola
Cello

a. _____

b. _____

c. _____

d. _____

OPEN STRINGS   SOUNDS

1. ☐   as written

2. ☐   as written

3. ☐   as written

4. ☐   8va lower than written

Activities for
GETTING TO KNOW THE PERCUSSION

© 1987 by Parker Publishing Company, Inc.

Name _____

Date _____

Score _____

Class _____

USE THE PICTURE CLUES   4–41

Fold this paper back on the dotted line. Study the names and shapes of these woodwind instruments. When you think you know the spellings, turn the page over and name as many instruments as you can to match the statements. Then unfold the paper and correct your answers.

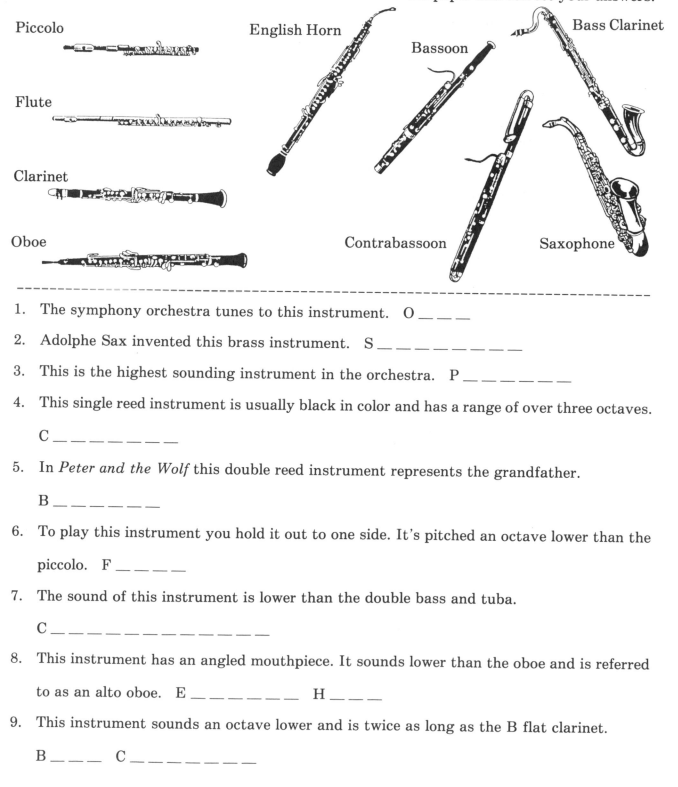

Piccolo

Flute

Clarinet

Oboe

English Horn

Bassoon

Bass Clarinet

Contrabassoon

Saxophone

- -

1. The symphony orchestra tunes to this instrument. O _ _ _ _

2. Adolphe Sax invented this brass instrument. S _ _ _ _ _ _ _ _

3. This is the highest sounding instrument in the orchestra. P _ _ _ _ _ _ _

4. This single reed instrument is usually black in color and has a range of over three octaves.

    C _ _ _ _ _ _ _

5. In *Peter and the Wolf* this double reed instrument represents the grandfather.

    B _ _ _ _ _ _ _

6. To play this instrument you hold it out to one side. It's pitched an octave lower than the

    piccolo. F _ _ _ _ _

7. The sound of this instrument is lower than the double bass and tuba.

    C _ _ _ _ _ _ _ _ _ _ _ _

8. This instrument has an angled mouthpiece. It sounds lower than the oboe and is referred

    to as an alto oboe. E _ _ _ _ _ _ _   H _ _ _ _

9. This instrument sounds an octave lower and is twice as long as the B flat clarinet.

    B _ _ _   C _ _ _ _ _ _ _ _

Name _____   Score _____

Date _____   Class _____

WOODWIND FACTS   4–42

Read each sentence. Circle "Yes" if it tells something true about the instrument. Circle the letter under "No" if it tells something that is not true.

		Yes	*No*
1.	Woodwind instruments were invented long ago when it was discovered that a musical tone could be produced by blowing across a reed, causing the air to vibrate.	T	O
2.	The mouthpiece of both the clarinet and saxophone uses one thin reed.	I	T
3.	Covering the holes of a woodwind instrument with the fingers shortens the distance the air travels, thus raising the pitch.	I	D
4.	The only instruments that use a double reed are the English horn, bassoon, contrabassoon, and oboe.	E	T
5.	The contrabassoon is the lowest sounding instrument of the orchestra.	S	O
6.	When a symphony orchestra tunes up, it tunes up to the oboe playing a "B flat."	N	S
7.	The oboe is the same length as a flute.	E	S
8.	The English horn is an alto oboe and can really sound a fifth higher.	I	U
9.	The saxophone is more likely to be used in a band than in a symphony orchestra.	G	S
10.	The B flat clarinet is twice as long as the bass clarinet and sounds an octave lower.	I	U
11.	The only members of the woodwind family held sideways are the flute and piccolo.	O	H
12.	The flute is a small piccolo, and is pitched an octave higher than the piccolo.	T	Y

Name _____ Score _____

Date _____ Class _____

KNOW YOUR RECORDER

10. To play the recorder, place the mouth-piece one-____ inch in your mouth.

11. The fingers should be slightly ____.

15. Keep the inside of the wooden instrument as ____ as possible.

16. To completely cover the holes, use only ____ pressure.

17. The ____ you hold or blow into the instrument affects its tone.

18. The tenor recorder is an octave ____ in pitch than the soprano recorder.

19. The soprano is higher in pitch than the alto, ____, or bass recorder.

DOWN

2. Blow an ____ flow of air into the recorder.

4. What syllable is said while playing the recorder?

6. ____ should not be raised.

8. The left ____ finger is not used on the recorder.

9. When playing, relax your ____.

12. As with any other instrument, ____ practice is important.

13. The ____ thumb is used to cover the hole on the underside.

14. Take the recorder apart with a ____ twisting motion.

17. A recorder may be made of ____ or plastic.

ACROSS

1. The underside of the instrument has ____ hole(s).

3. The ____ recorder is pitched a fifth lower than the soprano recorder.

5. There are ____ holes at the top of the instrument.

7. Only one finger is used on each ____.

Activities for
LEARNING ABOUT THE VOICE

Name _____

Score _____

Date _____

Class _____

DRAW THE SINGERS

4–44

For each block choose the section with the right number of ovals to match the word below. To show your answer draw in the faces and make them singing.

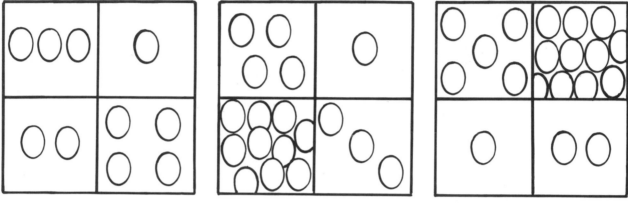

1. QUARTET   2. TRIO   3. ENSEMBLE

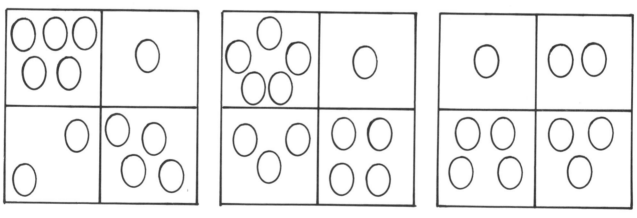

4. SOLO   5. QUINTET   6. DUET

MAKING BODY SOUNDS   4–45

Use your voice as your instrument and your body as the rhythm to make body sounds. Think of different types of sounds you can make with your mouth, tongue, lips, voice, fingers, hands, arms, legs, and feet. Draw pictures to illustrate the sound and write the descriptions underneath. The first one is done for you.

Tongue Clicking

GET WITH IT   4-46

You can tell by looking at these choir members that each has a problem. The director has been telling them constantly to "get with it." Their problems can be solved. Pretend that you are giving advice. Match each of the statements below with one of the choir members by writing the number under each.

1. Place your feet on the floor with the weight of your body somewhat forward, not leaning on the back of the chair. Sit up straight, but fairly relaxed.

2. Place the weight of your body toward your toes, not back on your heels. Roll your shoulders back.

3. Open your mouth and use your lips more in pronouncing the words. Remember to pronounce the final consonants distinctly.

4. Use an open, relaxed throat with a sensation that you are about to yawn. Sing with your mouth opened wide.

5. Throw away the gum.

6. Hold your music at eye level to project your voice outward instead of looking downward.

Name _____   Score _____

Date _____   Class _____

VOICE THE FACTS   4–47

These facts about the singing voice all have a word that is missing one or more letters. Fill in the blanks to complete the words by using any of the letters from the C Major Scale.

1. The singing voi __ __ is like a combination of a wind and stringed instrument with emotion and feeling.

2. The sound comes from the vibration of a pair of membranes or bands in the throat, called the vo __ __ l chords.

3. The vibrations are caused by air from the lun __ s that passes through a slit in the throat.

4. The vocal chords are stretched across the opening in the thro __ t to the larynx.

5. The pitch of the voice is controlled by muscles that tighten and relax the vocal __ hor __ s.

6. Another name for the voice box is the l __ rynx.

7. When the chords are stretched tight and thin, there are more vibrations and the pitch of the tone becomes hi __ h __ r.

8. When the vocal chords are relaxed, they become closer and thicker making the voice low __ r.

9. Vocal chords of men are about one and one-half times as long as those of wom __ n.

10. When singing, it is necessary to use the mus __ l __ s around the entire midsection of the body, not only the diaphragm.

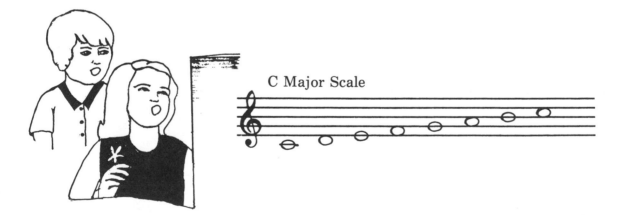

C Major Scale

NUMBER THEIR MUSIC 4–48

Match each singer with a description by writing the number on the singer's music.

1. Male voice, low register
2. Female voice, high register
3. Male voice, medium register
4. Female voice, low register
5. Male voice, high register
6. Female voice, medium register

WHAT'S THE RANGE?   4–49

Below are listed four different voice types. Write the type of voice on the blank to match the voice range.

Soprano
Alto
Tenor
Bass

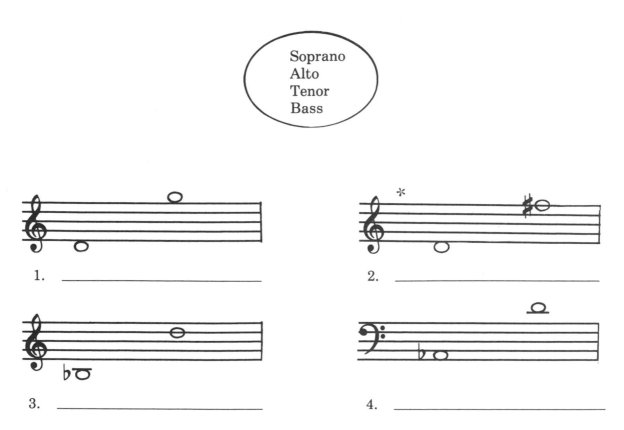

1. _____   2. _____

3. _____   4. _____

*Sounding one octave lower than written

Name _____

Date _____

Score _____

Class _____

DISTRIBUTE THEIR MUSIC

4–50

Help the conductor distribute the choir music by writing the number of the appropriate music on each member's folder.

Hallelujah

Handel

(8va lower)

1 Hal - le-lu-jah!

2 Hal - le-lu-jah!

3 Hal - le-lu-jah!

4 Hal - le-lu-jah!

Answer Key
for *Musical Instruments and the Voice*

4-1 SEE MY CUBBY!

Pictures will vary.

4-2 DREAMING

Pictures will vary.

4-3 DO I FIT THE INSTRUMENT?

This activity is self-checking.

4-4 DO I QUALIFY?

This activity is self-checking.

4-5 LIST THE BOOKS

Answers will vary.

4-6 CHART THE INFORMATION

Piano

   a. clef: treble and bass clefs are used.

   b. characteristics: The piano is a keyboard instrument with strings struck by hammers when keys are depressed. There are usually 88 keys.

   c. instrumentalist: (Encourage students to name an instrumentalist they know. That person might be a classmate or a famous musician like Artur Rubinstein or Oscar Peterson.)

Guitar

   a. clef: treble

   b. characteristics: A six-stringed instrument played by plucking the strings; used mainly in folk or popular music.

   c. instrumentalist: (answers will vary)

Clarinet

   a. clef: treble

   b. characteristics: A woodwind instrument with a mouthpiece using a single reed.

   c. instrumentalists: (answers will vary)

4-7 NOW AND THEN

1 (18th-century flute) matches with 6 (present-day flute).

2 (early European fiddle called a rebec) matches with 8 (present-day violin).

4 (zither) matches with 5 (present-day chromaharp or autoharp).

7 (17th-century primitive clarinet called a chalumeau) matches with 3 (present-day clarinet).

As a follow-up, you might ask the students to write the names under the present-day instruments. Provide the names of the older instruments.

4–8 SEAT THE ORCHESTRA

This activity is self-checking.

4–9 TUNING UP THE ORCHESTRA

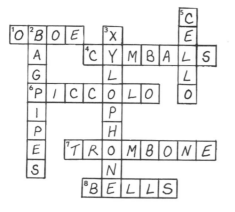

```
P O Ⓢ I L D A E M N O R C W P X E U P M A
G H M Y Z Ⓒ O N C E R T M A Ⓢ T E R M U V
I Q E Ⓑ M B R U M K M T O R T L K J I T A
Ⓟ M U A D P C X U T Ⓘ N S T R U M E N T Ⓢ
I Ⓣ G S U D H J M D E A M L I W Z Y M E T
T J U S V W E O E Y Ⓘ N T O N A Ⓣ I O N E
C E N N E R S U N I Q X T G G M W U X Y P
H I N N E D T M A Y P Y N W Ⓢ X I A N E O
D I W A E E R X Y C N Ⓒ O N C E R T Q E D
M C E I O D A Ⓦ O O D W I N D Z Y I E Y Ⓢ
```

4–10 PICTURE PUZZLE #1

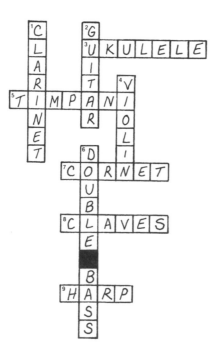

4–11 PICTURE PUZZLE #2

4-12 PICTURE PUZZLE #3

4-13 THE MISSING PART

1. The mouthpiece belongs to the saxophone (c).
2. The scroll belongs to the double bass (b).
3. The mouthpiece belongs to the trumpet (b).
4. The mallet belongs to the triangle (a).

Here is a breakdown of the families of instruments pictured in this activity:

Woodwind—1.	a. oboe	b. English horn	c. saxophone
String— 2.	a. harp	b. double bass	c. viola or violin
Brass— 3.	a. cornet	b. trumpet	c. French horn
Percussion—4.	a. triangle	b. tambourine	c. guiro

4-14 WHAT'S MISSING?

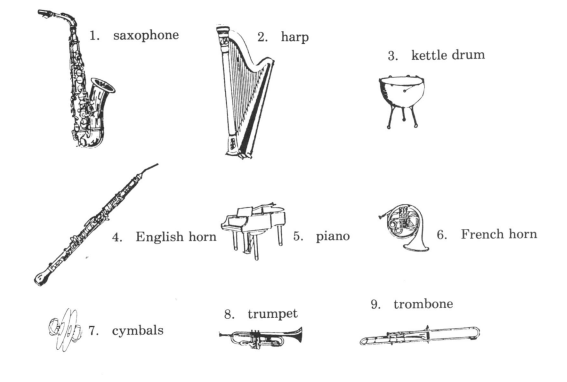

1. saxophone
2. harp
3. kettle drum
4. English horn
5. piano
6. French horn
7. cymbals
8. trumpet
9. trombone

4–15   WHAT'S THE MISSING SYLLABLE?

1. trom (trombone)
2. bag (bagpipe)
3. o (oboe)
4. or (organ)
5. cel (cello)
6. ban (banjo)

4–16   FIND THE MEMBERS

1. a, c, e
2. a, d, e
3. a, d
4. d, e
5. a, b

The names of the pictured instruments are:

1. a. tambourine   b. bugle   c. drums   d. ukulele   e. triangle
2. a. double bass   b. kettledrums   c. maracas   d. violin   e. viola
3. a. organ   b. banjo   c. chimes   d. piano   e. bassoon
4. a. flute   b. English horn   c. bells or glockenspiel   d. trumpet   e. tuba
5. a. saxophone   b. clarinet   c. gong   d. French horn   e. trombone

4–17   BRING IT ALONG

The items in the suitcase from left to right are:
reed, mute, drum sticks, bow (top of suitcase)

1. kettledrums—drum sticks****
2. violin or viola—bow***
3. clarinet—reed (part of mouthpiece)**
4. trumpet—mute*

4–18   WHAT'S IN COMMON?

1. e
2. d
3. g
4. f
5. c
6. b
7. h
8. a

4–19   NAME THREE

Suggested answers are:

1. violin, viola, cello, double bass
2. oboe, English horn, bassoon, contrabassoon
3. clarinet, bass clarinet, saxophone
4. violin, viola, trumpet, cornet, French horn, piano (soft pedal)
5. kettledrums, chimes, most percussion instruments, double bass
6. piano, organ, harpsichord, harp, cello
7. violin, viola, cello, double bass, harp, guitar, ukulele, balalaika, piano
8. trumpet, cornet, French horn, tuba, sousaphone, bugle, euphonium, trombone
9. kettledrum, bongo, tom-tom drum, hand drum
10. glockenspiel, xylophone, metallophone, various drums, wood block, temple blocks
11. synthesizer, piano, organ, marimba, xylophone, melodeon (harmonium)
12. violin, viola, cello, double bass
13. ukulele, guitar, balalaika, autoharp, mandolin
14. timpani, kettledrums, bass drum, harp, piano

15. kettledrum, timpani, bass drum, side drum, snare drum
16. triangle, wood block, tone block, gong
17. tambourine, triangle, cymbals, gong
18. guitar, organ, synthesizer, electronic keyboard

4-20 WHAT'S THE DIFFERENCE?

1. flute
2. piccolo } The piccolo is a small flute, pitched an octave above the flute.

3. viola
4. violin } The viola is tuned a fifth lower than the violin and is 1/7 larger in size than the violin.

5. oboe
6. English horn } The English horn is an alto oboe, pitched a fifth below the oboe.

7. clarinet
8. bass clarinet } The bass clarinet in B flat is pitched an octave lower than the B flat clarinet. The lower end of the bass clarinet is curved upward and the mouthpiece downward to make playing it easier.

4-21 MAKE UP YOUR MIND

1. X
2. O
3. O
4. X
5. O
6. O
7. O
8. O
9. X

4-22 CHOOSE THE MUSIC

1. h
2. c
3. t
4. i
5. p

The answers spell the word "pitch" reading from bottom to top.

4-23 HELP DETECTIVE BRASSO

1. T H (R) E E
2. T R O M B (O) N E
3. M U (T) E
4. T (R) U M P E T
5. B U G L (E)
6. (H) O R N
7. T U B (A)
8. B A (S) S
9. (C) O R N E T

Mystery word: ORCHESTRA

4-24 NOTE THE BRASS

1. tuba
2. bugle
3. trombone
4. French horn
5. sousaphone
6. cornet
7. tuba
8. trombone
9. bugle
10. cornet
11. sousaphone
12. French horn

4–25 BRASS FACTS

1. D (yes)
2. I (no)
3. K (no)
4. T (yes)
5. R (no)
6. A (yes)
7. M (yes)
8. S (no)
9. Y (yes)
10. R (no)
11. E (yes)
12. V (no

Explanation of *no* answers:

2. The trombone uses a slide, not valves.
3. The trombone is made of two brass tubes that are used like a telescope.
5. The smallest brass instrument is the trumpet.
8. The French horn is made from 12 to 16 feet of tubing.
10. The tuba plays the lowest tones, not the highest.
12. The trumpet player must also use the valves.

The answers spell "very smart kid" reading from bottom to top.

4–26 PIANO CARE QUIZ

1. sustain
2. horizontal
3. regularly
4. dampness
5. harmful
6. humidity
7. humidifier
8. playing
9. closed
10. retuned
11. cleaned
12. piano's

4–27 THE PIANO PUZZLE

1. KEYS, PATTERN
2. KEYBOARD
3. LONGER
4. INDICATES, HAND
5. LOWER, BASS, LEFT
6. FINGERING, HELPFUL

Statement: THE BLACK KEYS ARE ARRANGED IN GROUPS OF TWOS OR THREES.

4–28 A SYNTHESIZER STICKLER

1. pitch, tone, volume, and articulation all electronically
2. are produced by an oscillator
3. the more frequently the sound wave vibrates
4. harmonic frequencies in order to shape the sound
5. attack, sustain, decay, and release
6. ADSR
7. can memorize an entire musical line
8. more than one note at a time
9. synthetic music
10. by computer

4–29 MAKE YOUR OWN

Answers will vary.

4–30 CREATE A RHYTHM SCORE

Select one of the student's completed rhythm scores for a small group or the entire class to perform. Decide on $\frac{2}{4}$ or $\frac{4}{4}$ time. Practice the score, then perform as an accompaniment to a song using that particular meter. Write a repeat sign at the end of the score and continue playing until the music has stopped. As an additional help, measures could be numbered from 1 to 16.

4–31 DECODE THE PERCUSSION INSTRUMENTS

1. sand blocks
2. cowbell
3. wood block
4. castanets
5. tambourine
6. triangle
7. cymbals

4–32 STRICTLY STRIKERS AND SHAKERS

Suggest to the students that they use the "Word List" for the correct spellings.

4–33 SHENANIGANS

You might ask the students to name and classify the instruments on this activity sheet. The names of the instruments from left to right are given in parentheses:

1. BOOMING: bass drum is circled
   (sand block, glockenspiel, castanets, bass drum, jingle bells, claves)
2. RINGING: the bell is circled
   (snare drum or side drum, bell, bongo drum, field drum, tone block)
3. TAPPING: the rhythm sticks are circled
   (jingle bells, rhythm sticks, cymbals, chimes, tambourine, finger cymbals)
4. TINKLING: the triangle is circled
   (triangle, stick castanet, guiro, kettledrum, tone block)
5. RATTLING: the maracas are circled
   (cowbell, whip, hand drum, xylophone, maracas)

4-34   PERCUSSION FACTS

1. NO
2. NO
3. YES
4. NO

5. YES
6. YES
7. NO
8. NO

9. YES
10. YES
11. NO
12. YES

Explanations of *no* answers:

1. The bass drum varies in size, both in depth and in diameter.
2. The beaters for the snare drum are called drum sticks and are made of wood.
4. Another name for the timpani is kettledrum.
7. The crashing sound would probably be the cymbals.
8. Gypsy music makes use of the finger cymbals, castanets, and tambourines.
11. Gourds with peas or beans inside are called maracas. Castanets are clappers made of hard wood and in the shape of a shell. They are connected with a string.

4-35   A STRING OF MULTIPLE CHOICES

1. I
2. N
3. T
4. E
5. L
6. L
7. I
8. G
9. E
10. N
11. T

The answers reading down spell "intelligent."

4-36   GETTING INTO THE STRING OF THINGS

1. sound
2. loose
3. four
4. viola
5. bow

6. horse hair
7. frog
8. bow
9. bowed
10. two

11. across
12. violin
13. cello
14. octave

4-37   GUITAR GRAMMAR

1. Tuning Keys
2. Head
3. Nut
4. Fret
5. Neck

String 1 is E
String 2 is B
String 3 is G
String 4 is D
String 5 is A
String 6 is E

4-38 STRING FACTS

1.	F	(yes)
2.	I	(no)
3.	N	(yes)
4.	E	(no)
5.	A	(yes)
6.	N	(no)
7.	D	(no)
8.	D	(no)
9.	A	(no)
10.	N	(yes)
11.	D	(no)
12.	Y	(yes)

Explanation of *no* answers:

2. The double bass usually plays the bass line.
4. This technique of plucking can be done on almost any string instrument.
6. There are 43 strings on a harp and only 7 pedals.
7. The opposite is true.
8. The violin is the soprano of the string family.
9. The strings of the cello are one octave lower than those of the viola.
11. The strings of the cello are thinner than those of a bass.

The answers reading down spell "fine and dandy."

4-39 MATCH THE PARTS WITH THEIR NAMES

1. F
2. I
3. N
4. G
5. E
6. R
7. B
8. O
9. A
10. R
11. D

Identify the fingerboard as the part of a stringed instrument that you press the strings against to vary the pitch.

The answers reading down spell "fingerboard."

4-40 IT'S TUNE-UP TIME

1. violin (b)
2. viola (d)
3. cello (c)
4. double bass (a)

4-41 USE THE PICTURE CLUES

1. Oboe
2. Saxophone
3. Piccolo
4. Clarinet
5. Bassoon
6. Flute
7. Contrabassoon
8. English horn
9. Bass clarinet

4-42 WOODWIND FACTS

1. T (yes)
2. I (yes)
3. D (no)
4. E (yes)
5. S (yes)
6. S (no)
7. E (yes)
8. U (no)
9. G (yes)
10. U (no)
11. O (yes)
12. Y (no)

The answers reading up spell "You guessed it."

Explanation of *no* answers:

3. Covering the holes lengthens the distance and will lower the pitch.
6. The oboe plays an A to which the orchestra tunes.
8. The English horn sounds a fifth lower.
10. The opposite is true. The bass clarinet is twice as long as the B flat clarinet and it sounds an octave lower.
12. The opposite is true. The piccolo is a small flute, pitched an octave higher than the flute.

4-43 KNOW YOUR RECORDER

4-44 DRAW THE SINGERS

1. d
2. d
3. b or a or d

   (an ensemble is usually considered a group of vocal or instrumental musicians)

4. b
5. a
6. b

4-45 MAKING BODY SOUNDS

Answers will vary.

4-46 GET WITH IT

3, 1, 4, 5, 6, 2

4-47 VOICE THE FACTS

1. voice	5. chords	8. lower
2. vocal	6. larynx	9. women
3. lungs	7. higher	10. muscles
4. throat		

The letters for the C Major Scale from left to right are:

C   D   E   F   G   A   B   C

4-48 NUMBER THEIR MUSIC

Back row: Tenor (5), Baritone (3), Bass (1)
Front row: Soprano (2), Mezzo Soprano (6), Alto (4)

4-49 WHAT'S THE RANGE?

1. Soprano	3. Alto
2. Tenor	4. Bass

4-50 DISTRIBUTE THEIR MUSIC

Soprano (4), Alto (3), Tenor (1), Bass (2)

Clefs for Commonly Used Instruments and Voices

𝄞	This is the G clef. This clef points to G located on the second line. Notice how the curved line of the clef draws a ring around the second line. A staff with this clef is called the Treble Staff. The treble staff is most commonly used for general classroom music instruction. Children's singing voices and typical classroom instruments use this clef.

Clef Name Treble Clef or G Clef	These instruments use the treble clef:			
	Strings	*Percussion*	*Wind*	*Voices*
	Guitar	Piano (right	Cornet	Children's
	Ukulele	hand)	Trumpet	Singing voices
	Banjo	Xylophone	Flugelhorn	Soprano (Female)
	Violin	Chimes	French horn	Alto (Female)
	Harp	Glockenspiel	Tenor Trombone	Tenor (Male)
		Vibraphone	Euphonium	
		Marimba	Piccolo	
			Flute	
			Oboe	
			Clarinet	
			Alto Clarinet	
			Bass Clarinet	
			Bassoon	
			English Horn	
			Saxophone	

𝄢	This is the F clef. The "head" of the clef rests on the fourth line, which is F. The other notes run in order up and down the staff, with G in the space above F, and so on. A staff with this clef is called the Bass Staff. The bass staff is used for some men's singing voices and various instruments, including the left hand for keyboard instruments.

Clef Name Bass Clef or F Clef	These instruments use the bass clef.			
	Strings	*Percussion*	*Wind*	*Voices*
	Cello	Piano (left	Bassoon	Bass (Male)
	Bass	hand)	Contrabassoon	
	Harp	Timpani	French Horn	
		Marimba	Trombone	
			Tuba	

Progress Chart for
Musical Instruments and the Voice

Use this chart to keep a record of activities completed for each class. List your classes (or students) in the given spaces at the right. As each activity is completed for a class, mark an "X" in the appropriate column.

Activity Number/Title		Skill Involved				

Self-Assessment

4-1	SEE MY CUBBY!	Drawing a favorite instrument				
4-2	DREAMING	Drawing an instrument of the future				
4-3	DO I FIT THE INSTRUMENT?	Naming an instrument by reading the requirements to play it				
4-4	DO I QUALIFY?	Naming an instrument by reading the requirements to play it				

Library Research

4-5	LIST THE BOOKS	Listing and classifying books on instruments of the orchestra				
4-6	CHART THE INFORMATION	Researching various musical instruments				
4-7	NOW AND THEN	Matching old-fashioned instruments with ones currently in use				

Band, Orchestral, and Folk Instruments

4-8	SEAT THE ORCHESTRA	Completing a seating chart for the modern symphony orchestra				
4-9	TUNING UP THE ORCHESTRA	Reading for comprehension on how the orchestra tunes				
4-10	PICTURE PUZZLE #1	Naming instruments from picture clues				
4-11	PICTURE PUZZLE #2	Naming instruments from picture clues				

Activity Number/Title	Skill Involved				
		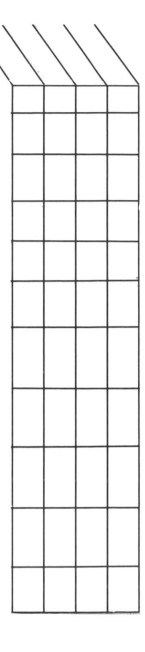			
4-12 PICTURE PUZZLE #3	Naming instruments from picture clues				
4-13 THE MISSING PART	Circling instruments that have missing parts				
4-14 WHAT'S MISSING?	Naming instruments and drawing their missing parts				
4-15 WHAT'S THE MISSING SYLLABLE?	Using picture clues to identify instruments				
4-16 FIND THE MEMBERS	Matching instruments to their families				
4-17 BRING IT ALONG	Classifying instruments and drawing missing items				
4-18 WHAT'S IN COMMON?	Deciding what related instruments have in common				
4-19 NAME THREE	Naming three instruments that have one thing in common				
4-20 WHAT'S THE DIFFERENCE?	Naming and explaining differences in sets of instruments				
4-21 MAKE UP YOUR MIND	Categorizing instruments according to one's position while playing				
4-22 CHOOSE THE MUSIC	Matching instruments to their range in pitch				

Getting to Know the Brass

		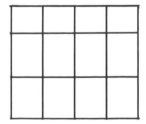			
4-23 HELP DETECTIVE BRASSO	Writing words to complete brass definitions				
4-24 NOTE THE BRASS	Naming brass instruments by using notation code				
4-25 BRASS FACTS	Deciding if brass statements are true or false				

Getting to Know the Keyboard

		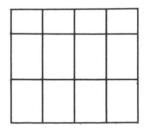			
4-26 PIANO CARE QUIZ	Completing sentences about piano care				
4-27 THE PIANO PUZZLE	Using a code to complete statements about the piano				
4-28 A SYNTHESIZER STICKLER	Completing sentences about synthesizers				

Activity Number/Title		Skill Involved
Getting to Know the Percussion		
4–29	MAKE YOUR OWN	Designing rhythm instruments
4–30	CREATE A RHYTHM SCORE	Writing a rhythmic composition
4–31	DECODE THE PERCUSSION INSTRUMENTS	Identifying percussion by description and decoding
4–32	STRICTLY STRIKERS AND SHAKERS	Writing names of percussion instruments
4–33	SHENANIGANS	Classifying percussion instruments
4–34	PERCUSSION FACTS	Testing knowledge of percussion instruments

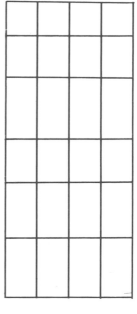

Getting to Know the Strings		
4–35	A STRING OF MULTIPLE CHOICES	Completing sentences about stringed instruments
4–36	GETTING INTO THE STRING OF THINGS	Testing knowledge of stringed instruments
4–37	GUITAR GRAMMAR	Identifying and matching strings and parts of a guitar
4–38	STRING FACTS	Deciding if string statements are true or false
4–39	MATCH THE PARTS WITH THEIR NAMES	Identifying parts of a stringed instrument and bow
4–40	IT'S TUNE-UP TIME	Identifying stringed instruments and matching to their open strings

Getting to Know the Woodwinds		
4–41	USE THE PICTURE CLUES	Identifying woodwind instruments from descriptions
4–42	WOODWIND FACTS	Deciding if woodwind statements are true or false
4–43	KNOW YOUR RECORDER	Recalling facts about the recorder

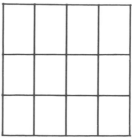

Activity Number/Title		Skill Involved	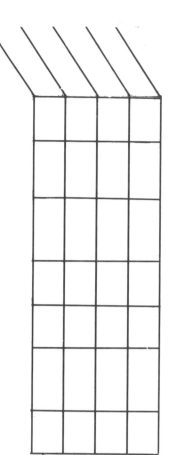

Learning About the Voice

4-44	DRAW THE SINGERS	Drawing correct number of singers to match the type of ensemble
4-45	MAKING BODY SOUNDS	Illustrating body and mouth sounds and writing descriptions
4-46	GET WITH IT	Matching descriptions to improve choir members' problems
4-47	VOICE THE FACTS	Completing words to finish statements about the voice
4-48	NUMBER THEIR MUSIC	Matching voice type with the description
4-49	WHAT'S THE RANGE?	Writing voice type and matching with its range in pitch
4-50	DISTRIBUTE THEIR MUSIC	Matching singers to pitch range on vocal scores

Types of Musical Instruments
and the Voice

THE VOICE

Soprano
Alto
Tenor
Baritone
Bass

THE ORCHESTRA

WOODWIND SECTION

Piccolo   Clarinet
Flute   Bass Clarinet
Oboe   Bassoon
English Horn   Contrabassoon

BRASS SECTION

(French) Horn
Trumpet
Trombone
Tuba

STRING SECTION

Violin
Viola
Cello or Violoncello
Double Bass, Contrabass,
   String Bass, Bass Viol, or Bass
Harp

PERCUSSION SECTION

Definite Pitch

Timpani or Tympani
Xylophone
Glockenspiel (orchestra bells)
Chimes (tubular bells)
Marimba

Indefinite Pitch

Snare Drum or Side Drum
Bass Drum
Cymbals
Triangle
Gong or Tam-Tam
Castanets
Woodblock
Chinese or Temple Blocks

Latin American
Percussion Instruments

Clavés   Bongos
Maracas   Timbales
Guiro

SPECIAL INSTRUMENTS OF THE ORCHESTRA

Celesta
Harpsichord
Piano

OTHER INSTRUMENTS OF THE ORCHESTRA OR BAND

Alto Clarinet—Woodwind Section
Saxophone—Woodwind Section
Bugle—Brass Section
Cornet—Brass Section
Euphonium—Brass Section
Flügelhorn—Brass Section
Vibraphone—Percussion Section
Kettledrums—Percussion Section

PRE-BAND INSTRUMENTS

Melodicas
Melody Bells
Autoharp or Chromaharp
Electronic Keyboard
Metallophone
Resonator Bells
Flutaphone
Songflute
Tonette
Recorder
Ukulele

CLASSROOM MUSIC RHYTHM INSTRUMENTS

Hand Castanets	Cowbell
Stick Castanets	Jingle Bells
Finger Cymbals	Rhythm Sticks
Hand Drum	Sand Blocks
Tom-Tom Drum	Tone Block
Tuneable Drum	

COMMONLY USED FOLK INSTRUMENTS

Bagpipe	Guitar
Balalaika	Mandolin
Banjo	

COMMONLY USED KEYBOARD INSTRUMENTS

Electric Organ	Synthesizer
Pipe Organ	

Name _____

Date _____

Craft Project
for *Musical Instruments and the Voice*

ACCORDION MUSIC BOOKS

Objective: The purpose of this activity is to give students a highly motivating independent activity in which they name, describe, and illustrate various instruments and classify the different types of singing voices.

Materials Needed:

- Construction paper
- Scissors
- Ruler
- Colored pencils
- Pencil or pen
- Rubber band
- *Optional:* Magazine pictures of instruments or people singing
- *Optional:* Paste

Construction Directions:

1. Cut the construction paper four or five inches wide and as long as possible. Measure off four- or five-inch squares on the strips and fold the paper accordion style.
2. After the accordion book has been folded with the number of pages desired, draw pictures (or use magazine pictures) of instruments and/or voices. Suggested subjects include string, woodwind, brass, percussion, keyboard, orchestra, band, folk instruments, and different types of singing voices.
3. On the page opposite the picture, write a brief description of the instrument or that particular type of singing voice. Then use a rubber band to hold the book together.

Uses:

1. Categorize the instruments by families or types in the book.
2. After the students become familiar with different families of instruments, have them select a family for further study to use for constructing an "Accordion Music Book."
3. Provide an opportunity for students to explore different musical instruments of various countries or different cultures. Record their findings along with illustrations in an "Accordion Music Book."
4. After the books are completed, provide listening experiences for the students to identify visually which instrument is being heard. Have the students find that particular page in their book.
5. Beginners might construct the "Accordion Music Book" by illustrating and describing such classroom instruments as rhythm sticks, tambourines, castanets, and triangles.
6. Encourage students to use their music vocabulary to describe instruments and the voice.
7. Develop students' familiarity with different voice types by having them write verbal descriptions and illustrate the correct gender, or cut out pictures of male and female singers.

Incentive Badges

To the teacher: Cut apart badges and keep in a handy 3″ × 5″ file box along with tape. Encourage students to write their names and the date on the backs of their badges and to wear them.

For hopping to it!
Good helper badge
in music class.

Best in the class.....
MUSIC AWARD

MUSIC CLASS AWARD

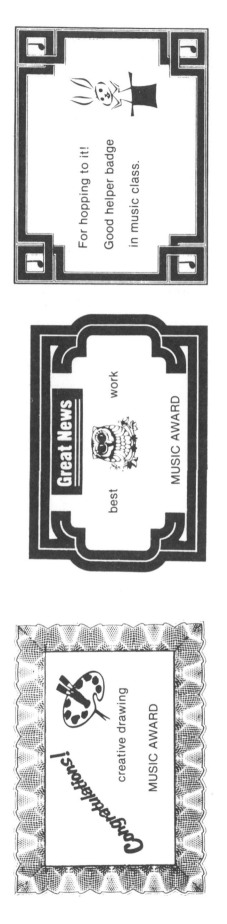

best   work

MUSIC AWARD

DOG GONE GOOD
MUSIC AWARD!

(name)

to
MUSIC CLASS

creative drawing

MUSIC AWARD

Best performer
in
Music Class!

MUSIC SHARE-A-GRAM

TO: _____ DATE _____
(Parent's Name)

FROM: _____ SCHOOL _____
(Classroom Music Teacher)

RE: _____ CLASS _____
(Student's Name)

To help you recognize your child's success in music class or any area that needs attention the following observation(s) has/have been made.

	Exceptional	Satisfactory	Unsatisfactory
Shows musical aptitude			
Shows creativity			
Shows talent			
Shows initiative			
Self-concept in music class			
Fairness in dealing with classmates			
Self-direction			
Care of instrument and equipment			
Reaction to constructive criticism			
Observes music class rules			
Starts and completes work on time			
Generally follows directions			

over for comments ▶

RETURN-A-GRAM

TO: _____ DATE _____
(Classroom Music Teacher)

FROM: _____ SCHOOL _____
(Parent's Name)

RE: _____ CLASS _____
(Student's Name)

Please write your comments or questions on the back and return. If you want to be called for a parent-teacher conference, indicate below.

_____ Class _____ Year _____

_____
(Student's Name)

STUDENT RECORD PROFILE CHART

Select the appropriate data in parentheses for each category, i, ii, iii, and iv, and record the information in the chart below as shown in the example.

i.—Unit Number for *Music Curriculum Activities Library* (1, 2, 3, 4, 5, 6, 7)

ii.—Date (Day/Month)

iii.—Semester (1, 2, 3, 4) or Summer School: Session 1 (S1), Session 2 (S2)

iv.—Score: Select one of the three grading systems, a., b., or c., that applies to your school progress report and/or applies to the specific activity.

a.

(O)	= Outstanding
(G)	= Good
(S)	= Satisfactory
(NI)	= Needs Improvement
(U)	= Unsatisfactory
(I)	= Incomplete
(—)	= Absent

b.

(A)	= 93–100 [percentage score]
(B)	= 85–92
(C)	= 75–84
(D)	= 70–74
(F)	= 0–69
(I)	= Incomplete
(—)	= Absent

c.

(R/P):	
R	= Correct number of responses.
P	= Possible correct number of responses.
(I)	= Incomplete
(—)	= Absent

i	ii
iii	iv

Student's Name _____ Class _____ Year _____

MUSIC SELF-IMPROVEMENT CHART (for student use)

a. On the back of this chart write your goal(s) for music class at the beginning of each semester.
b. On a separate sheet record the date and each new music skill you have acquired during the semester.

c. MUSIC SHARE-A-GRAM (date sent to parent)

d. RETURN-A-GRAM (date returned to teacher)

e. MUSIC AWARD BADGES (date and type rec'd)

1.
2.
3.

f. SPECIAL MUSIC RECOGNITION (date and type rec'd)

1.
2.
3.

g. SPECIAL MUSIC EVENT ATTENDANCE RECORD (date and name of special performance, recital, rehearsal, concert, field trip, film, workshop, seminar, institute, etc.)

1.
2.
3.
4.

h. ABOVE AND BEYOND: Extra Credit Projects (date and name of book report, classroom performance, construction of hand-made instrument, report on special music performance on TV, etc.)

1.
2.
3.
4.

i. PROGRESS REPORT/REPORT CARD RECORD (semester and grade received)

1.
2.
3.
4.

j. MUSIC SIGN-OUT RECORD (name of instrument, music, book or equipment with sign-out date and due date)

1.
2.
3.
4.
5.
6.
7.
8.
9.
10.

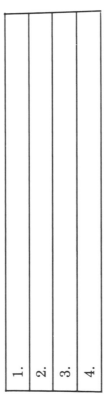

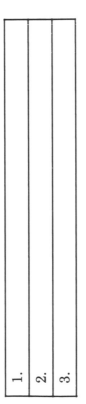

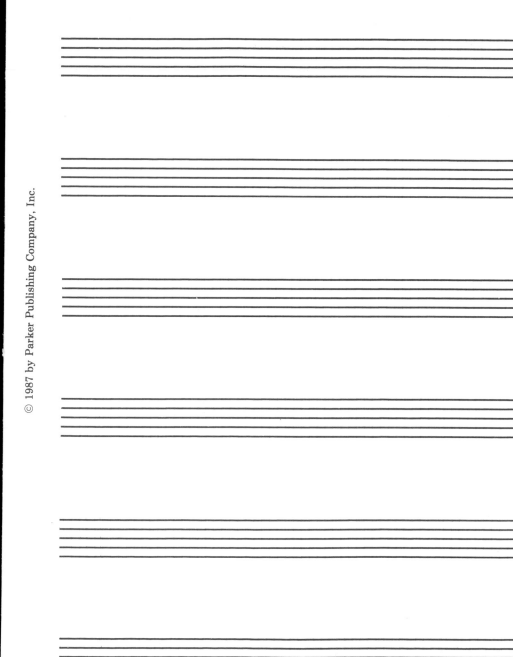